Introduction

A lifelong passion for food.

One of my earliest memories is of my mother and I making blackberry tarts together at the kitchen table. Being only about three years old, I had to stand on a stool where I spent a lot the time saying that I needed more berries or pastry and I loved every moment of it!

We lived in the country and only went into town about once a month; during these trips I would visit every shop that sold cooking utensils and gadgets and I pestered the staff with questions about what each implement was for. Not living close to shops meant that we had to be self-sufficient, and my grandmother, who was a superb cook, maintained an amazing vegetable and herb garden. From her I not only learned a great many cooking techniques, but also how to preserve and pickle fruit and vegetables for use during the winter months.

Our house was close to a small fishing village and many of my relations were fishermen, a tradition carried on today by their sons and grandsons. Having fishermen in the family meant that we had an abundance of fresh fish, and when the weather permitted I learned how to prepare and cook fresh seafood from an early age. The most important lesson was that really fresh fish (straight off the boat) only needed some seasoning, a few herbs and a minimum of cooking to taste absolutely fantastic. Realising that good quality, fresh ingredients didn't need much help to bring out their flavours has helped me immensely during my cooking career.

In school I won many of the cookery competitions and felt that I had a talent for it. I decided to train as a chef when I left school and although the work was very hard I thoroughly enjoyed the experience. The buzz and creativity of a busy kitchen is something very special and has to be experienced first-hand to be believed.

After thirteen years of marriage and three children we moved to Ryeland House, which is situated on a farm a few miles outside Kilkenny city. We had very little money and my uncle Roy, who was involved with the food industry, encouraged me to earn some money by teaching people to cook. Many of my first students were friends of mine who came along to support my new business and in 1991 this gave birth to Ryeland House Cookery.

Since then I have been teaching people of all ages and abilities to cook; everyone from Transition Year boys and housewives to career women who want to entertain at home. I do hope you enjoy cooking the recipes in this book as much as I have enjoyed putting them together.

Dedication

I dedicate this book to my long suffering husband Pat, who has always supported me in my endeavours.

Acknowledgements

For many years I have been encouraged by my sister Clare to write a cookbook. Now on completion, though challenging, I enjoyed the experience. Thank you Clare for your encouragement.

I have many people to thank who helped in various different ways.

My good friend and colleague, Edward Hayden, for every ounce of energy and encouragement with this book - you are a gentleman! Carol Marks, my chosen photographer, your attention to detail was overwhelming. You have done a brilliant job and really kept us motivated on the shoot - thank you Carol! Tim Casey, you initially designed my web but became my coordinator and mentor, your kindness, friendship and generosity are deeply appreciated. To Claire and Valerie of Claire Goodwillie Design, thank you for your patience with me and your expertise.

No list of acknowledgements would be complete without further thanks to Alma and Sally, my two wonderful assistants in Ryelands. To all my foodie and good friends who had to listen to me for months rattling on about my book. To my mother Maria who's direction in life was wonderful and to Axel Nijland, thank you for the use of your beautiful Irish dresser. A big thank you to Niall, Adam and Alan, students of CBS, Callan. With his keen editorial eye, Philip Watson went above and beyond the call of a good friend throughout this whole process with his epic job of proof reading. Also to Fiona at the Kilkenny County Enterprise board for all her help and encouragement.

The beautiful youngsters that appear in this book are my wonderful neighbour's children; Ailish, Joe and Maria Lalor, and none other than my granddaughter, Eva.

Finally, my husband and my three children, you have endured many a conversation and consultation about my book – thank you for always listening.

Contents

Abbreviations used in this book

Tablespoon	tbsp		Gram	g
Kilogram	kg		Litre	l
Millilitre	ml		Pound	lb
Teaspoon	tsp		Ounce	oz
Dessertspoon	dsp		Fluid ounce	fl oz
Pint	pt		Centigrade	C

Standard spoon measures are level.
1 tsp = 5ml, 1 dsp = 10ml, 1 tbsp = 15ml.

Metric to Imperial Conversion

Quantities in this book are given in both metric and imperial measurements. An exact conversion from imperial to metric measures does not usually give very convenient working quantities so the metric measurements have been rounded down to units of 25 grams. The table below shows the recommended equivalents

When converting quantities over 20oz first add the appropriate figures in the central column and then adjust to the nearest unit of 25. For example, suppose we want to convert a weight of 27oz, we would add 198 (value for 7oz) and 567 (the value for 20oz) to get 765. The nearest unit of 25 to 765 is 775, so for a weight of 27 oz we would use 775g. As a rule of thumb, 1kg (1000g) is equal to 2.2lb

This conversion technique gives adequate results for most recipes but for some pastry and cake recipes a more exact conversion needs to be done to get a perfectly balanced recipe.

It is important to use either imperial or metric measurements, do not use both in the same recipe as they are not interchangeable.

WEIGHT CONVERSION	Imperial (ounces)	Approximate grams to nearest whole figure	Recommended conversion to nearest unit of 25
	1	28	25
	2	57	50
	3	85	75
	4	113	100
	5	142	150
	6	170	175
	7	198	200
	8 (½ lb)	227	225
	9	255	250
	10	283	275
	11	312	300
	12	340	350
	13	368	375
	14	396	400
	15	425	425
	16 (1 lb)	454	450
	17	482	475
	18	510	500
	19	539	550
	20 (1 ¼ lb)	567	575

LIQUID MEASURE CONVERSION	Imperial	Approximate ml to nearest whole figure	Recommended ml
	1/4 pt	142	150ml
	1/2 pt	283	300ml
	3/4 pt	425	450ml
	1 pt	567	600ml
	1 ½ pt	851	900ml
	1 ¾ pt	992	1000ml (1 litre)

Herbs and Spices

Basil	Oregano or thyme
Chervil	Tarragon or parsley
Chive	Spring onion, onion or leek
Coriander	Parsley
Italian Seasoning	A blend of any of the following: basil, oregano, rosemary and ground red pepper.
Marjoram	Basil or thyme
Mint	Basil, marjoram or rosemary
Oregano	Thyme or basil
Parsley	Chervil or coriander
Poultry Seasoning	Sage and a blend of any of the following: thyme, marjoram, savory, black pepper and rosemary.
Red Pepper	A dash of bottled hot pepper sauce or black pepper
Rosemary	Thyme or tarragon
Sage	Poultry seasoning, marjoram or rosemary
Savory	Thyme, marjoram or sage
Tarragon	Chervil, fennel seed or aniseed
Thyme	Basil, marjoram or oregano
Allspice	Cinnamon, cassia, a dash of nutmeg or mace or a dash of cloves
Aniseed	Fennel seeds or a few drops of anise extract
Cardamom	Ginger
Chilli Powder	A dash of hot pepper sauce and a combination of oregano and cumin.
Cinnamon	Nutmeg or allspice (only use ¼ stated amount)
Cloves	Allspice, cinnamon or nutmeg
Cumin	Chilli powder
Ginger	Allspice, cinnamon, mace or nutmeg
Mace	Allspice, cinnamon, ginger or nutmeg
Nutmeg	Cinnamon, ginger or mace
Saffron	A dash of turmeric (to add colour)

Ann's Spice Advice

Dried spices Dried spices should be stored in airtight containers in a cool, dark place. When buying dried spices only buy small amounts at a time, this will help ensure that they will be used quickly. The flavour of dried spices lessens with age and spices that are old or no longer fragrant are of little use. Check the spices in your store cupboard and discard those that are past their best.

Along with salt, black pepper is one of the most commonly used flavourings. It is at its best when freshly ground because it looses its flavour very quickly. It is used in many recipes and can also be used to enhance the flavour of fruit such as strawberries and pineapple.

Chilli flakes Crushed dried red chillies can be used to add extra bite to many dishes from pasta sauces to salads. Add chilli flakes gradually to a dish, you can always add more if needed but you cannot take them out.

Cayenne pepper This is good in cheese dishes, creamy soups and sauces. It is made from a hot type of red chilli so use carefully.

Paprika Paprika is used in many Spanish dishes and is a vital ingredient in Hungarian goulash. It has a slightly sweet taste and is available in both a hot and mild form.

Saffron Saffron has a distinct but delicate flavour and is used sparingly in many types of dishes such as paella, curry, risotto, etc. Saffron strands have the best flavour and are most effective when infused in a little hot liquid such as milk or water.

Cumin Cumin is widely used in Indian and North African dishes. It works well with meat and a variety of vegetables.

Coriander This spice is widely used in both Indian and Asian cooking and is often combined with cumin. It is available whole or ground and is delicious with meat especially lamb. Ground coriander and cumin make a great spice rub.

Turmeric Turmeric is a bright yellow spice with a slightly earthy, peppery taste that is used in many Indian dishes. It is made from the ground, dried turmeric root.

Salt Salt is probably the most important seasoning used in cooking. The type of salt selected for use is important; rock or sea salt contain no added chemicals such as the anti-caking agents found in table salt. Sea salt is slightly stronger in taste and is typically used in smaller amounts. Rock salt is available in crystal form and can be ground in a mill or refined to produce cooking salt.

Cinnamon Available in stick form or ground into a powder this spice is used in both savoury and sweet dishes. Ground cinnamon is used in baking, drinks and desserts. Cinnamon in its stick form can be added to stews, casseroles and other liquid dishes and removed before serving.

Nutmeg	Nutmeg has a spicy flavour that enhances the taste of spinach and adds a warm spiciness to milk, egg and cream dishes. It is available ready-ground but has a far better flavour if freshly ground.
Mace	Mace has a similar, though milder, taste to nutmeg and is made from the seed casing of the nutmeg. It is good for flavouring butter for use in savoury dishes.
Allspice	This spice is most commonly found in its ground form and has a slightly warm cinnamon-clove taste. It can be used in both savoury and sweet dishes and is particularly suited to fruit cakes and winter recipes.
Cloves	These dried flower buds are available in both whole and ground form and can be used in savoury and sweet dishes. The ground spice is suitable for cakes and cookies. Whole cloves are often used in hot drinks such as mulled wine and are magnificent when used to stud a glazed ham before baking. Ground cloves have a very strong flavour so use with a light hand.
Vanilla	Vanilla comes in a variety of forms from vanilla extract and vanilla essence to dried vanilla pods (beans) which are long and black in colour. The dried vanilla pods contain hundreds of tiny seeds. To use vanilla pods, warm the whole pod in milk or place in a sealed jar of sugar, which allows the flavour to infuse the milk or sugar. The pods can also be split open and the seeds scraped out (using the point of a knife) and added to ice cream, cakes and desserts. Vanilla extract is distilled from the vanilla pods and makes a good substitute for vanilla pods. However the pods have a better flavour than vanilla extracts which can have a strong flavour.
Lemongrass	Lemongrass is excellent with fish and chicken and can also be used to flavour sweet dishes such as ice cream. It can be used in a variety of ways; the stalk can be finely chopped or sliced and stirred into a dish or alternatively the bulbous end can be bruised or crushed and added whole to a curry or soup.
Garlic	The strength of flavour of garlic depends very much on how it is prepared. The most powerful flavour is achieved by crushing the cloves of garlic. A simple technique for crushing garlic is to place the clove under the blade of a broad bladed knife and to push down on it on a solid surface. Obviously extreme care should be taken when using knives and especially when crushing garlic in this way. A slightly less powerful flavour can be achieved by slicing, shredding or chopping the cloves of garlic. Garlic can be used to flavour salad dressings, dips, can be roasted for a milder flavour and whole peeled cloves can be used to flavour oils or vinegars.
	The smell of garlic can linger on the breath; chewing fresh parsley is said to counteract this.
Fresh root ginger	Fresh root ginger is brown in colour and should be peeled before being finely chopped, grated, sliced or shredded for use. It is used in stir-fries, curries and many other dishes. When buying select plump roots, they can be stored in the fridge for up to 6 weeks. Ginger is also used in sweet dishes in its preserved or crystallised form.
	Fresh root ginger gives a fresh flavour to savoury recipes and drinks while dried ginger is particularly useful for baking.

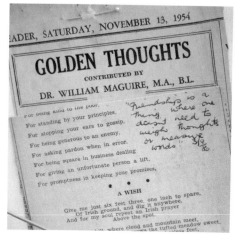

Family Food Made Easy

In today's busy world families don't spend as much time together as they used to. A family meal is always a good time to spend together discussing the events of the day or week and even for arguing a little!. Family meals should be simple, easy to cook food that tastes delicious. Relaxed, uncomplicated cooking is central to comfortable family gatherings and a big dish made ahead of time lets you fully enjoy the occasion.

Family Food Made Easy

Chilli Potato Tart
with Sun-dried Tomatoes, Roasted Garlic and Chillies

Serves 4

Total cooking time approx 1 hour 10 minutes

This tart makes a brilliant vegetarian option and is always requested by my vegetarian friends when they are invited over for dinner. Its good enough to satisfy even the most committed meat eater.

Ingredients

- 3 red chillies, or to taste, cut lengthways and deseeded
- 8 cloves of garlic, peeled
- 2 tablespoons of olive oil
- 28 semi sun-dried tomatoes
- 6 ripe beef tomatoes, cored
- 6 large waxy potatoes, thinly sliced
- 600ml (approx. 1 pt) full fat milk
- 1 pastry case, blind baked
- 4 tablespoons of crème fraiche
- 2 tablespoons of grated Parmesan cheese
- ½ teaspoon sweet paprika
- A small bunch of basil

Method

Preheat the oven to 200C / 180C fan-oven / Gas mark 6.

Chop the beef tomatoes into 6 or 8 pieces, depending on size. Place the pieces into a roasting tray and bake in the preheated oven for 40 minutes. Drain off the liquid (which is good for soup). This process intensifies the flavour and reduces the moisture content.

Toss the chillies and the 6 cloves of garlic in olive oil, place on a roasting tray and roast for 10 minutes. Remove from the oven and put them into a liquidiser with 20 of the semi sun-dried tomatoes. Blitz the ingredients briefly to give a rough puree.

Reduce the oven setting to 170C / 150C fan-oven / Gas mark 3.

Cook the sliced potatoes in the milk with the 2 remaining cloves of garlic until just tender. Discard the milk or use as a base to make soup.

Spread the chilli mixture over the pastry base, cover with the well drained beef tomatoes and season well. Layer the sliced potatoes on top seasoning as you go, leaving a 6cm gap at the edge.

Spoon the crème fraiche over the potatoes, sprinkle over with the grated Parmesan and return to the oven for 20 minutes.

Remove and dust with the paprika. Allow to cool for about 15 minutes and then decorate with the remaining semi sun-dried tomatoes and basil leaves. The basil can be brushed with olive oil which gives the leaves a shiny, bright appearance.

Tomato, Pepper and Mozzarella Tart

Serves 4-6
Total cooking time approx 1 hour

Keep a packet of frozen pastry in the freezer for emergencies; combined with stock ingredients from your store cupboard it can be very useful for those unexpected guests!

Ingredients

For the tart

- 1 x 375g sheet of ready-made puff pastry, thawed if frozen
- 1 large red pepper
- 1 large yellow pepper
- 2 cloves of garlic, peeled and crushed
- 3 tbsp of olive oil
- 4 heaped tbsp of pesto, homemade or from a jar
- 150g (approx. 5oz) of mozzarella, drained and thinly sliced
- 125g (approx. 4 ½ oz) red cherry tomatoes, halved and stalks removed
- 125g (approx. 4 ½ oz) yellow cherry tomatoes, halved and stalks removed
- ½ tsp dried oregano or marjoram
- 1 egg, beaten
- 25g (approx. 1oz) Parmesan cheese, grated or shaved
- Basil leaves
- Sea salt and ground black pepper

Method

Preheat the oven to 200C / 180C fan-oven / Gas mark 6.

Remove the pastry from the fridge at least 20 minutes before you need to unroll it.

Quarter the peppers, remove the inside and then cut each quarter in half lengthways. Place the sliced peppers in a roasting dish with the garlic, pour over 2 tbsp of olive oil and mix together well. Roast for 20-25 minutes or until the edges of the peppers begin to blacken. Remove from the oven and leave to cool for 10 minutes.

Unroll the pastry and lay it on a large, buttered baking tray. Using a sharp knife, score a line around the sheet of pastry about 1 ¼ cm in from the edge.

Spread the pesto evenly over the pastry inside the scored line. Lay the strips of pepper across the base of the tart on top of the pesto alternating red and yellow sections.

Arrange the slices of mozzarella over the peppers and season with salt and black pepper. Evenly arrange the halved tomatoes over the mozzarella sprinkle the dried oregano over the tart, season again and drizzle over the remaining olive oil.

Increase the oven temperature to 220C / 200C fan-oven / Gas mark 7.

Brush the edges of the tart with the beaten egg and bake for 12 minutes or until the edge of the tart is well puffed up and beginning to brown.

Reduce the oven temperature to 200C / 180C fan-oven / Gas mark 6 and cook the tart for another 12-15 minutes or until the tips of the tomatoes are well browned.

Sprinkle the Parmesan over the tart and set aside to cool for about 5 minutes. Scatter the basil leaves over the tart to finish and serve warm.

Special Chicken Stew

Serves 4

Total cooking time approx 70 – 75 minutes

This recipe is based on the classic French fricassee of chicken. A fricassee means flavoured meat fried and turned into a stew, using flour as a thickening agent. In this recipe I have adapted an original recipe using individual spring chickens, but you can use a jointed whole chicken if desired.

Ingredients

- Salt and freshly ground black pepper
- 4 spring chickens or poussins
- 1 small handful of fresh parsley, leaves picked, stalks kept
- 1 bunch of fresh tarragon, leaves picked, stalks kept
- 4 teaspoons wholegrain mustard
- 2 heaped tablespoons of plain white flour
- Extra virgin olive oil
- 1 white onion, peeled and finely chopped
- 2 cloves of garlic, peeled and finely sliced
- ½ celery heart, trimmed back and finely sliced
- 2 good knobs of butter
- 2 wine glasses of crisp white wine
- 600ml (approx. 1 pt) of stock
- 3 gem lettuces, quartered
- 1 small bunch of seedless grapes, washed and halved

Anne's Tip

A fricassee can also be successfully made using white fish

Method

Preheat the oven to 180C / 160C fan-oven / Gas mark 4.

Season the baby chickens inside and out and stuff each with the parsley and tarragon stalks. Using your forefinger, carefully part the skin from the breast meat and smear a teaspoon of the wholegrain mustard into each bird. Rub the flour over the chickens so that they are covered in a thin layer. Keep any flour that falls off.

In a snug-fitting casserole-type pan fry your chickens over a high heat in 3 good lugs of olive oil on all sides for about 10 minutes until golden. Remove them to a plate and fry off the onion, garlic and celery in the pan.

Add the butter and the retained flour and continue to fry for about 4 minutes, scraping off any goodness that is on the bottom of the pan. Pour in the 2 glasses of white wine and allow the liquid to reduce by half before returning the chickens to the pan.

Next, pour in stock until the level of liquid reaches about half-way up the chickens. Make yourself a paper lid, wet the paper to make it flexible then tuck it in and around the pan.

Place in the oven and cook for about 50 - 60 minutes until the chickens have crisp skin and the thigh meat falls off the bone.

Remove the chickens to some nice serving bowls, ones that can hold some sauce, and place the pan back on the hob. Add the lettuces, grapes, parsley leaves and tarragon leaves and simmer for a couple of minutes. Correct the seasoning carefully and serve beside the chicken in each bowl.

Luxury Cottage Pie

Serves 6
Total cooking time approx 1 hour

This is comfort food at its best, great for the family on cold winter days or those evenings when you don't want to put too much effort into putting a meal together.

Ingredients

- 900g (approx. 2lb) potatoes, peeled and cut into chunks
- 1 medium egg, beaten
- 25g (approx. 1oz) of butter
- 3-4 tbsp milk
- 700g (approx. 1 ½ lbs) beef mince
- 1 onion, peeled and chopped
- 2 carrots, peeled and diced
- 2 tbsp plain flour
- 150ml (approx. ¼ pt) red wine
- 300ml (approx. ½ pt) beef stock
- 1 (400g) tin of chopped tomatoes
- 2 tbsp fresh chopped thyme
- 1 tsp Worcestershire sauce

Method

Preheat the oven to 200C / 180C fan-oven / Gas mark 6.

Cook the potatoes in a pan of boiling, lightly salted water for 15-20 minutes until tender. Drain, return to the pan and mash well. Add the egg, butter and milk, mash again until smooth and fluffy. Season with salt and freshly ground black pepper and set aside.

Heat a pan until hot; add the minced beef and cook, stirring, for about 5 minutes until browned. Add the chopped onions and carrots, cook for another 3 minutes until they start to soften.

Sprinkle the flour over the cooked mince and cook for another minute, stirring constantly. Add the wine, stock, tomatoes, thyme and Worcestershire sauce; stir the mixture while bringing it to the boil. Season and then reduce the heat, simmer for 15 minutes.

Transfer the mince mixture to a large ovenproof dish, spoon the mashed potatoes on top, spread out and fluff up the mash potato using a fork.

Bake in the preheated oven for 30-35 minutes until golden, serve hot.

Chicken in Fragrant Sauce

Serves 4
Total cooking time approx 20 minutes

This dish is extremely easy and can be served with boiled rice for the busy cook.

Ingredients

- 4 chicken breasts, boneless and skinless
- 1 tablespoon runny honey
- 2 tablespoons of sunflower oil
- 1 onion, very thinly sliced
- 1 tablespoon of curry powder
- 1 tablespoon of brandy
- 300ml (approx. ½ pt) double cream
- 2 tablespoons of mango chutney
- The juice of ½ a lemon
- Salt and freshly ground black pepper
- 1 tablespoon of chopped, fresh parsley

Method

Slice the chicken breasts lengthways into large strips and toss in the honey.

Heat 2 tablespoons of the oil in a large non-stick frying pan and brown the chicken strips all over (you may need to do this in batches), set aside.

In the unwashed frying pan heat the remaining oil, add the onions and fry over a medium heat for about 10 minutes or until softened.

Sprinkle the curry powder over the onions, pour in the brandy and stir. Mix in the double cream and return the chicken strips to the pan.

Cover the pan and simmer over a low heat for about 5 minutes or until the chicken is cooked through. Stir in the mango chutney and lemon juice and season well. Serve on boiled rice sprinkled with the chopped parsley.

Steak and Kidney Pie

Serves 6
Total cooking time approx 2 hours

My grand daughter Eva just loves this pie which she calls "Mac's pie" because some of my friends call me "Mac".

Ingredients

- 5 tbsp of plain flour
- 900g (approx. 2lb) braising beef, cut into cubes
- 220g (7oz) beef kidney, remove the membrane and cut into chunks
- 600ml (approx 1pt) stock
- 1 tbsp Dijon mustard
- 15g (approx. ½oz) of butter
- 225g (approx. 8oz) shallots, trimmed and peeled
- 500g (approx. 1lb 2oz) puff pastry, defrost if frozen
- Beaten egg to glaze

Method

Place the plain flour on a plate and season the flour generously with salt and freshly ground black pepper. Dredge the beef and chopped kidney through the seasoned flour to coat, do in batches and set aside.

Heat the butter and oil in a large frying pan, add the onions and cook, stirring occasionally for 8-10 minutes until the onions begin to soften and turn golden brown. Remove the onions from the pan using a slotted spoon and set aside.

Fry the flour coated meat in the frying pan, adding extra oil if necessary, over a high heat for 4-5 minutes until browned on all sides.

Place the meat and onions in a large, deep saucepan or flameproof casserole dish; pour over the stock and stir in the mustard. Bring to the boil, then reduce the heat, cover and simmer for about 1 ½ hours stirring occasionally. Top up with extra stock if needed and cook until the meat is just tender. Transfer the meat and liquid to a 1.2 litre (2 pt) pie dish and cool for 20 minutes.

Preheat the oven to 220C / 200C fan-oven / Gas mark 7.

Roll the pastry out to a size slightly greater than the size of the dish containing the meat. If you have a pie funnel place it in the centre of the dish (these can be purchased in any good cook's shop). Dampen the rim of the dish with water and place the pastry over the top. Press the edges well to seal, trim off the excess pastry and knock up edges using the back of a knife. Cut the pastry trimmings into diamonds, mark with leaf veins and place on pie to decorate. Brush the pastry with beaten egg and bake for 25-30 minutes in the preheated oven until well risen and golden. Serve with green beans.

Roast Leg of Lamb
with Garlic and Rosemary "Pesto"

Serves 6-8
Total cooking time approx 1 ½ – 2 ½ hours depending on how well the meat is cooked

You can't beat a good roast for providing the most satisfying meals that people always enjoy. When my children were away at college one of them would always ring on a Friday morning asking for a "real" dinner that night i.e. a roast and veg.

Ingredients

- 2.5kg (approx. 5 ½ lb) leg of lamb
- 2 sprigs of fresh rosemary, leaves picked and roughly chopped
- 3 cloves of garlic
- 2 tbsp of olive oil
- 1 tsp plain flour
- 600ml (approx. 1pt) of fresh lamb or chicken stock, hot

Method

Preheat the oven to 230C / 210C fan-oven / Gas mark 8. For medium (pink) lamb cook for approximately 1 ½ hours, for well-done lamb cook for 2 ¼ - 2 ½ hours.

Using a small sharp knife, make small 2.5cm (1in) deep slits all over the leg, about 5cm (2in) apart.

Make the garlic and rosemary "pesto". Put the rosemary leaves, garlic, ½ teaspoon of salt and some freshly ground black pepper into a mini food processor or spice grinder. Turn on the machine and slowly add enough oil to make a smooth paste.

Push some of the "pesto" into each of the slits you made in the leg of lamb, rub any of the remaining paste and oil on the outside of the leg. Season the joint lightly with a little more salt and pepper.

Put the lamb, rounded side up, into a roasting tin and roast in the oven for 15 minutes. Lower the oven temperature to 200C / 180C fan-oven / Gas mark 6 and continue to roast for the remainder of the calculated roasting time. For a 2.5kg leg cooked to medium (so the meat is pink near the bone), you need to roast the lamb for a further 1-1 ½ hours.

When the lamb has cooked to your liking, remove from the oven and lift it onto a carving board or large plate, cover it tightly with a sheet of foil. Leave the meat to rest for 15-20 minutes before you start carving.

While the meat is resting make the gravy. Pour away the excess fat from the roasting tin and place the tin with the lamb juices over a medium heat on the hob. Sprinkle with the flour and stir for a few moments with a wooden spoon. Gradually add the stock and scrape up all the caramelised juices from the bottom of the tin. Leave to simmer gently until it has reduced to a well flavoured gravy then strain into a gravy boat. Adjust the seasoning if necessary and keep hot.

Carve the lamb into slices and serve immediately with the homemade gravy. Roast lamb goes wonderfully with creamy dauphinoise or roast potatoes and steamed fine green beans.

Rhubarb and Ginger Cake Upside-down

Serves 8
Total cooking time approx 35 minutes

Rhubarb is easily grown so if you have room in your garden why not sow a rhubarb stool. It will provide you with rhubarb the following year.

Ingredients

- 50g (approx. 2oz) of butter
- 250g (approx. 9oz) of brown sugar
- 450g (approx. 1lb) of rhubarb, trimmed and cut into 2cm pieces
- 200g (approx. 7oz) of self raising flour
- ½ tsp of baking powder
- ¼ tsp salt
- ¼ tsp of bicarbonate of soda
- 2 eggs, free range if possible
- 200ml (approx. 7 fl oz) of buttermilk
- 75ml (approx. 2 ½ fl oz) of sunflower oil
- 1 generous tsp of grated, fresh ginger

Method

Preheat the oven to 190C / 170C fan-oven / Gas mark 5.

Melt the butter in an ovenproof frying pan and stir in half of the sugar and cook over a gentle heat for 4-5 minutes. Add the rhubarb – there is no need to stir. Remove the frying pan from the heat and set aside.

Sift the flour, baking powder, salt and the bicarbonate of soda into a mixing bowl. Whisk together the eggs, remaining sugar, buttermilk, oil and ginger. Pour the liquid into the dry ingredients and mix well.

Pour the batter over the rhubarb then bake in the preheated oven for 30 minutes or until the cake feels firm. Put a plate on top of the pan and turn out. Serve with crème-fraiche or whipped cream.

Apple and Sultana Crumble

Serves 6

Total cooking time approx 40 - 45 minutes

This is a fantastic autumn dish that makes great use of the apple harvest.

Ingredients

- 900g (approx. 2lb) cooking apples, peeled, cored and chopped
- 2 tbsp lemon juice
- 100g (approx. 4oz) sultanas or 150g (approx. 6 oz) raspberries/blackberries
- 75g (approx. 3oz) caster sugar
- 175g (approx. 6oz) plain flour
- 100g (approx. 4oz) butter, cubed
- 75g (approx. 3oz) Demerara sugar
- 75g (approx. 3oz) nuts such as hazelnuts, pecans or walnuts roughly chopped and roasted
- Custard to serve

Method

Preheat the oven to 180C / 160C fan-oven / Gas mark 4.

Place the chopped apples, lemon juice and sultanas in a large ovenproof dish. Sprinkle the caster sugar over the fruit, mix well together and set aside.

Sift the flour into a large mixing bowl. Add the butter and rub in with your fingertips until the mixture resembles breadcrumbs. Continue to rub in until the mixture forms clumps.

Stir in the Demerara sugar and the nuts reserving 1 tbsp of both the sugar and nuts to use for the topping. Sprinkle the crumble mixture evenly over the fruit and scatter the reserved sugar and nuts over the top.

Bake in the preheated oven for 45-50 minutes until the crumble is a golden colour, serve with custard.

Raisin Bread and Butter Pudding

Serves 8
Total cooking time approx 40 - 45 minutes

I suppose we were reared on bread and butter pudding, my Mum would always use up leftover bread and have this ready for us when we arrived home from school.

Ingredients

For the pudding
- 50g (approx. 2oz) butter, softened
- 400g (approx. 1lb) of bread, crusts on
- 100g (approx. 4oz) raisins
- 500ml (approx. 1pt) milk
- 150ml (approx. ¼ pt) double cream
- The grated zest of 1 lemon
- 4 eggs
- 50g (approx. 2oz) golden caster sugar
- 2 tbsp brandy or 1 tsp vanilla extract

For the topping
- 2 tbsp Demerara sugar
- 2 tbsp chopped nuts
- 1 tsp ground cinnamon

Method

Preheat the oven to 190C / 170C fan-oven / Gas mark 5.

Butter a 2 litre shallow, ovenproof dish. Spread each slice of bread with butter and halve the slices diagonally.

Put the milk, cream and lemon zest into a saucepan. Slowly bring the mixture to the boil, and then cool until lukewarm.

Beat the eggs and sugar; add the brandy or vanilla essence and the warm lemon milk.

Arrange the bread, buttered side down, over the base of the buttered dish, sprinkle over half of the raisins. Repeat the bread and raisin layers and pour over the egg mixture. Allow the layers to soak for 15 minutes. The final layer should be buttered side up.

Mix the topping ingredients together and sprinkle over the pudding. Bake in the preheated oven for about 40-45 minutes until golden brown and firm.

Rest the pudding for about 5 minutes before serving. Serve with whipped cream or crème fraiche.

Easter Simnel Cake

This is a lusciously rich fruit cake with a layer of almond paste baked into the centre of the cake and decorated with an almond topping.

Total cooking time approx 2 – 2 ½ hours

Ingredients

For the Almond paste

- 350g (approx. 12oz) ground almonds
- 175g (approx. 6oz) caster sugar
- 175g (approx. 6oz) icing sugar
- 2 eggs to bind
- 1 tsp almond essence

For the cake

- 225g (approx. 8oz) butter
- 225g (approx. 8oz) caster sugar
- 4 large eggs
- 225g (approx. 8oz) plain flour
- 1 ½ tsp baking powder
- 1 tsp mixed spice
- 225g (approx. 8oz) sultanas
- 225g (approx. 8oz) raisins
- 50g (approx. 2oz) candied peel, chopped

To Decorate

- 1 tbsp apricot jam
- 1 small egg, beaten

Method

Preheat the oven to 150C / 135C fan-oven / Gas mark 2. Prepare a 20cm (8in) cake tin by lining the sides and base with grease proof paper, brush the grease paper with melted butter.

To make the almond paste put the almonds and caster sugar into a bowl, sieve in the icing sugar and mix together. Beat 2 eggs lightly with the almond essence, stir enough of the beaten eggs into the almond and sugar mixture to form a stiff but pliable paste. Roll out about a third of the almond paste into a circle that is just slightly less than 20cm (8in). Wrap the remaining paste in clingfilm and set aside to use for the cake topping and decoration.

For the cake mixture, cream the butter and sugar together until the mixture is a pale colour and is light and fluffy in texture. Add the beaten eggs alternating with the flour, baking powder and spices, when all have been mixed together stir in the fruit.

Put half the cake mixture into the prepared tin; lay the circle of almond paste gently on top and cover with the remaining cake mixture. Make a shallow hollow in the centre of the top layer of cake mixture but be careful not to press too heavily, otherwise the almond paste may fall to the bottom of the tin rather than being in the middle.

Bake the cake in the preheated oven for 2-2 ½ hours, then cover with a double thickness of non-slick bakewell paper and continue cooking until the centre of the cake is firm. When cooked, remove from the oven and leave to cool in the tin, after cooling remove the lining paper and decorate.

Increase the temperature of the oven to 200C / 180C fan-oven / Gas mark 6.

To decorate, roll out another third of the prepared almond paste to the same size as the top of the cake and warm the apricot jam. Brush the top of the cake with the warmed apricot jam and lay the almond paste carefully on top of the jam, press the almond paste gently into place. Level the almond paste with the help of a rolling-pin and neaten the edges.

Mark the top of the cake into small squares. Divide the remaining almond paste into eleven balls and (using a little apricot glaze) stick these at regular intervals around the edge of the cake.

Brush all the almond paste with a little beaten egg. Wrap several thicknesses of brown paper around the outside of the cake and return the cake to the oven for about 10 minutes until the almond paste is a light golden brown.

Fish

Fish is absolutely one of my favourite foods and has been throughout my life. There are a great many wonderful ways to cook fish, but whatever way you choose do take care not to overcook it. Fish is a tasty, nutritious food that lends itself to both the simplest and most exotic dishes. It can be used for light lunches or for more substantial, hearty dinners or suppers.

Fish

Crab Soup

Serves 4-6

Total cooking time approx 25 minutes

This is a light, refreshing crab soup with a hint of lemongrass.

Ingredients

- 25g (approx. 1oz) of butter
- 1 onion peeled and chopped
- 1 carrot, peeled and chopped
- 1 stick of celery, trimmed and chopped
- 1 stalk of lemongrass, trimmed and finely chopped
- 50g (approx. 2oz) of long grain rice
- 300ml (approx. ½ pt) of fish or chicken stock
- 600ml (approx. 1pt) of milk
- 225g (approx. 8oz) of crabmeat, white and brown
- 2 tbsp of Thai fish sauce
- 1 tbsp of finely chopped fresh parsley
- Salt and freshly ground black pepper

Method

Melt the butter in a large saucepan, add the onions, carrot, celery and lemongrass and cook for 3-4 minutes stirring occasionally. Take care that the vegetables do not burn.

Stir in the rice and cook for 1-2 minutes, then add the fish stock and milk and bring to the boil.

Reduce the heat and simmer for 15-20 minutes or until the rice and vegetables are cooked. Transfer to a liquidiser or blender and whiz to a puree.

Return the soup to the saucepan and stir in the crabmeat and fish sauce. Heat gently for about 5 minutes, taste and adjust the seasoning then add the chopped parsley.

Serve in large mugs or bowls.

Smoked Haddock Hash with Poached Eggs

Serves 6-8
Total cooking time approx 20 minutes

This is a perfect dish for a lazy Sunday brunch or lunch: it's filling, satisfying and tasty. Best of all it is very easy to prepare.

Ingredients

- 3 tbsp wine vinegar
- Salt
- 750g (approx. 1 ½ lb) smoked haddock fillet
- 55g (approx. 2oz) of butter
- 1 medium leek, trimmed and sliced
- ½ yellow pepper, diced
- ½ red pepper, diced
- 4 spring onions, finely sliced
- 500g (approx. 1lb 2oz) of potatoes, peeled and cut into 2cm (about 1in) cubes
- 2 tbsp light olive oil
- 2 tbsp parsley
- 200g (approx. 7oz) of mayonnaise
- 2-3 tbsp Dijon mustard
- 6-8 eggs, preferably free range

Method

Bring 2 litres (approx. 4 ½ pts) of water to the boil, add the vinegar and 1 tbsp of salt reduce to a simmer and poach the smoked haddock for 8-10 minutes then drain. When the fish has cooled enough, flake the flesh into 2 cm (approx. 1in) pieces.

Melt half of the butter in a large saucepan with 2 tbsp of water, and then add the leek, peppers, spring onions and a little salt. Cook over a moderate heat for 5 minutes until the liquid has evaporated and the vegetables have started to brown. Set aside.

In a large pan, fry the potatoes in olive oil until golden. Gently mix in the poached fish, vegetables and herbs then press down gently with a spatula. Dot the surface with the remaining butter, cover and cook gently for 5-7 minutes.

Mix the mayonnaise and mustard together.

Lightly poach the eggs in a wide pan of simmering water.

To serve, turn the hash out onto a large plate or divide out onto individual plates. Top each portion with a poached egg and serve with the mustard mayonnaise.

Anne's Tip
If smoked haddock is not readily available you can use smoked cod or coley instead.

Seafood Chowder

Serves 8
Total cooking time approx 10 minutes

Seafood chowder has always been the comfort food of choice in our house. It would be made whenever we received a delivery of fresh fish from our relatives in Wexford with some smoked fish added for extra flavour.

Ingredients

- 50g (approx. 2oz) of butter
- 2 onions, diced
- 2 leeks, diced
- 3 carrots, diced
- 3 large potatoes, diced
- 1 ½ tbsp of plain flour
- 450ml (approx. 1pt) of white wine
- 1 ½ litres (approx. 3pts) of chicken or fish stock
- 150g (approx. 5oz) of smoked salmon, skinned and cubed
- 150g (approx. 5oz) of smoked haddock, skinned and cubed
- 150g (approx. 5oz) of fresh cod, skinned and cubed
- 150g (approx. 5oz) of mussels
- 150g (approx. 5oz) of prawns
- 450ml (approx. 1pt) of cream
- Some parsley and dill
- Salt and pepper

Method

Melt the butter in a large, heavy-bottomed pot over a medium heat; add the onion, leeks, carrots and potatoes and sweat in the butter for about 5 minutes.

Add the flour and cook over a low heat for 2 minutes, stirring constantly. Slowly stir in the white wine followed by the stock, bring to the boil and simmer for 5 minutes.

Check the fish for bones, removing any you find, cut the fish into pieces and add to the soup. Let the soup simmer for about 10 minutes then stir in the cream. Taste and adjust the seasoning if necessary. Finally sprinkle in the chopped herbs.

Creamy Lentil Salad with Cured Salmon and Avocado

Serves 4

Total cooking time approx 30 minutes

My grandmother was a great cook and she was the one who introduced me to lentils at the tender age of six. Many years later I still love lentils, for their taste and for the memories of my grandmother that they evoke.

Ingredients

- 200g (approx. 7oz) of small lentils, such as Puy
- 1 red onion, finely chopped
- 1 tbsp red wine vinegar
- 2 tbsp extra virgin olive oil
- 2 sticks of celery, finely sliced
- 1 tomato, diced
- 2 tbsp of finely chopped, fresh flat leafed parsley
- 2 tbsp of finely chopped, fresh dill or chives
- 150g (approx. 5oz) of crème fraiche or low fat yoghurt
- 1 ripe avocado
- 300g (approx. 11oz) of cured (gravadlax) or smoked salmon, or both
- 50g (approx. 2oz) of wild rocket leaves

Method

Put the lentils and onion in a saucepan with about 750ml (about 1 ½ pt) of water. Bring to the boil and simmer for 20-30 minutes until the lentils are tender but not soft.

In a large bowl mix the vinegar and olive oil and season with sea salt and black pepper. Drain the lentils and onion, rinse in cold water and drain again.

Tip the rinsed and drained lentils into the bowl of vinegar dressing and toss lightly. Add the celery, tomato, herbs and crème fraiche or yoghurt and toss again.

Cut the avocado into quarters, peel and slice lengthways. Arrange the salmon slices on four plates and top with the creamy lentils, avocado slices and some of the rocket. Serve with lemon wedges if desired.

Seared Salmon or Cod
with Roasted Red Pepper Vinaigrette

Serves 4
Total cooking time approx 8 minutes

This dish is full of gutsy Mediterranean flavours, which contrast brilliantly with either salmon or cod.

Ingredients

- 1 red pepper, halved and deseeded
- 1 clove of garlic, peeled
- 2 tbsp of red wine vinegar
- 5 tbsp of olive oil
- A dash of Tabasco sauce or a pinch of cayenne pepper

For the salad

- 250g (approx. 9oz) of fine green beans, trimmed
- A handful of black olives, stoned
- A few torn basil leaves
- A few cherry tomatoes, halved
- 4 salmon or cod fillets
- A squeeze of lemon juice
- 150g (approx. 5oz) of watercress

Method

Preheat the oven to 200C / 180C fan-oven / Gas mark 6.

For the dressing, roast the pepper until charred, place it in a plastic bag or wrap in clingfilm until cool and remove skin. Place the peeled pepper in a food processor with the remaining dressing ingredients and whiz for 1 minute.

For the salad, blanche the green beans in boiling, salted water until just tender and then drain. While the beans are still warm add the dressing and stir through the olives, basil, tomatoes and then season well. Set aside.

Place the salmon or cod on an oiled baking tray and season with salt, pepper and lemon. Roast the fillets in the preheated oven for 6-8 minutes or until cooked to your liking.

To serve, divide the watercress between each plate, top with the salad, flake over the salmon or cod and drizzle over the dressing.

Fish Pie

Serves 6
Total cooking time approx 30 - 40 minutes

Cooking the potatoes with saffron gives them a beautiful colour and the flavour is perfect with fish. This fish pie has been a family favourite for many years, especially with my daughter who loves seafood.

Ingredients

For the topping

- 700g (approx. 1 lb 9 oz) of even sized potatoes, sliced
- A good pinch of saffron
- 25g (approx. 1oz) of butter

For the filling

- 500g (approx. 1 lb 2 oz) of cod fillets, skinned
- 200g (approx. 7oz) of smoked haddock
- 400g (approx. 14oz) of salmon fillets
- 100g (approx. 4oz) of frozen prawns
- 4 plum tomatoes
- 50g (approx. 2oz) of butter
- A 2.5cm (approx. 1in) piece of fresh root ginger, chopped
- 50g (approx. 2oz) of plain flour
- 425ml (approx. ¾ pt) of milk
- 150ml (approx. ¼ pt) of dry white wine
- 142ml carton of single cream
- 3 tbsp of chopped dill
- The juice of ½ a lime

Method

Preheat the oven to 200C / 180C fan-oven / Gas mark 6.

Check the fish for bones and remove any you find. Cut the cod, salmon and smoked haddock into 2.5cm (about 1in) pieces. Peel the tomatoes, cut in half, remove the seeds and then chop into pieces. Mix the fish, prawns and tomatoes and place into a buttered 2 litre (approx. 4pt) pie dish or other ovenproof dish (choose one that's not too shallow).

Put the butter, ginger, flour, milk and wine into a non-stick saucepan and bring slowly to the boil, whisking all the time until the sauce is thickened and smooth. Reduce the heat and simmer the sauce for 2 minutes, then season well with salt and pepper and remove from the heat. Leave the sauce to cool; stir occasionally to prevent a skin forming. When the sauce has cooled to room temperature stir in the cream.

Stir the dill and limejuice into the sauce, taste and adjust the seasoning if necessary. Pour the sauce evenly over the fish.

Peel and slice the potatoes, place them in a pot with enough water to cover and add the saffron and some salt. Bring to the boil, then cover and cook for 10-12 minutes until the potatoes are just tender. Drain well and leave until they are cool enough to handle.

Arrange the potato slices, overlapping, over the top of the pie mixture. Melt the butter and brush over the potatoes. Bake the fish pie for 30-40 minutes until the potatoes are crisp and golden.

Tagine of Arthurstown Mackerel

Serves 6
Total cooking time approx 1 hour

Mackerel are a seasonal fish best enjoyed while very fresh…less than 24 hours out of the sea if possible. Old mackerel are best left for the seagulls, or for use as bait. This dish is named after Arthurstown in County Wexford, where I spent my childhood. One of my great summer memories is running home with mackerel so fresh from the sea that they still wriggled. In those days we cooked them very simply, either fried in the pan or grilled.

This dish results from my love of travelling and learning about the great cuisines of the world. It is based on the Moroccan custom of cooking fish with chermoulah which is a spicy marinade. Different regions have their own versions and some are quite fierce with lots of chilli powder. The vegetables are cooked first and the fish is placed on top of the vegetables towards the end of cooking.

The cooked fish tastes delicious the next day and makes a great and unusual addition to a picnic.

Ingredients

- 6 mackerel fillets
- Chermoulah
- 4 large floury potatoes
- 4 carrots
- 4 ripe plum tomatoes, chopped
- 12 sun-dried tomatoes
- 2 cloves of garlic
- 6 tbsp of sunflower oil
- 4 tbsp of lemon juice
- 1 ½ tbsp of tomato puree
- 150ml (approx. 5 fl oz) of water
- Sea salt
- Fresh coriander, chopped to garnish

For the chermoulah

- The juice of 2 lemons
- 300ml (approx. 10 fl oz) of extra virgin olive oil
- 50g (approx. 2oz) of coriander, chopped
- 50g (approx. 2oz) of flat-leaf parsley, chopped
- 4 cloves of garlic, peeled and finely chopped
- 1 tbsp of ground cumin
- 1 tsp of ground coriander
- 1 tbsp of sweet paprika
- A pinch of chilli powder
- Sea salt and freshly ground black pepper

Method

To make the chermoulah, pour the lemon juice and olive oil into a mixing bowl. Add all the other ingredients and whisk well to combine.

Rub the mackerel fillets with salt and leave for about 12 minutes, this removes some of the moisture from the fish and helps to intensify the flavour. Rinse the salt off the fillets and pat dry with paper towel.

Place the fillets in a single layer in a shallow dish and pour over ½ of the chermoulah and rub it into the fish. Cover the dish and marinate the fish for at least 30 minutes.

Preheat the oven to 200C / 180C fan-oven / Gas mark 6.

Peel the potatoes and cut into 1 ½ cm (¾ in) cubes, peel the carrots and cut into pieces the same size as the potato cubes. Mix the remaining chermoulah with the tomato puree, lemon juice, oil and water. Stir the chopped vegetables into the chermoulah and place the mixture in a shallow ovenproof dish, large enough to accommodate the mackerel fillets.

Sprinkle the chopped garlic over the vegetables and scatter both the chopped tomatoes and sun-dried tomatoes over the top. Cover the dish tightly with tin foil and a lid if you have one. Place in the oven and bake for about 35-40 minutes, or until the vegetables are tender.

Uncover the vegetables and place the mackerel fillets on top, skin side up. Pour the remaining marinade mixture over the fish and bake in the oven for about 20 minutes or until the fish is cooked.

Allow the dish to cool slightly before serving; it should be warm rather than very hot. Scatter the chopped coriander over the top to garnish. This dish is excellent with couscous, especially when flavoured with the zest and juice of a lemon.

Pan Roasted Fillet of Hake with Creamy Curried Mussels

Serves 6
Total cooking time approx 15 minutes

Wild mussels grow in the bay that lies in front of my family home, and as children we were often dispatched with a bucket to harvest the freshest shellfish you could ever imagine. My love of sea fresh mussels continues to this day.

Ingredients

- 400g (approx. 14 oz) of mussels, scrubbed and beards removed
- 1 bay leaf and 2 sprigs of thyme
- 75ml (approx. 2 ½ fl oz) of white wine
- 3 tbsp of olive oil
- 2 carrots, finely diced
- 1 leek, white part only, finely diced
- 2 sticks of celery, finely diced
- 3 tsp of mild curry powder
- 3 pinches of saffron strands
- 450ml (approx. 1pt) of dry vermouth
- 450ml (approx. 1pt) of fish stock
- 450ml (approx. 1pt) of cream
- 6 x 225g (approx. ½ lb) fillets of hake
- 150g (approx. 5oz) of spinach, washed and shredded
- Sea salt and freshly ground black pepper

Method

Preheat the oven to 180C / 160C fan-oven / Gas mark 4.

Place the mussels, wine, thyme and bay leaf in a large saucepan and heat. Cover and steam for about 3-4 minutes, hold the lid firmly on the pot and shake every now and again. Uncover, remove any mussels that have not opened and discard them. Strain the cooking liquid and reserve. Remove the meat from the shells and also reserve.

In a clean pan heat the olive oil and add the carrot, leek and celery and cook over a gentle heat for 4-5 minutes. Add the curry powder and saffron and cook for another minute. Pour in the vermouth and continue cooking until the liquid has reduced down to a syrupy consistency.

At this stage add the stock and reserved mussel liquor and continue to cook until reduced by half. Add the cream and simmer for 5 minutes then season to taste.

Heat a little oil in an ovenproof pan, and when hot, add the hake fillets skin-side down. Cook the fillets over a high heat for 1-2 minutes, turn the fish over and then place the pan in the preheated oven and cook for a further 3-4 minutes.

While the fish is in the oven, finish the sauce by adding the meat from the mussels and the spinach; stir and simmer for about 2 minutes.

Divide the sauce between plates and top with the hake fillets. Serve immediately.

Simple Dishes for Transition Year Students

Transition year provides a great opportunity for students to gain the skills that will enable them to cope when they leave home to study or work. Being able to prepare tasty, nutritious meals and dishes is an essential skill; they can impress their friends with their cooking, have a healthier lifestyle and even save on their living expenses because fresh ingredients are cheaper and taste better than ready meals or fast food.

For more than TEN years the Transition Year boys from the CBS in Callan, Co. Kilkenny have been coming to Ryeland House for cooking lessons. They have proven to be very enthusiastic students, so much so, that several of them have pursued careers as chefs after finishing school.

Simple Dishes for Transition Year Students

Curried Parsnip Soup

Serves 4-6
Total cooking time approx 35 minutes

This is always a great favourite with students (especially boys) who enjoy the unique flavour that the curry paste adds; it is certainly different from the usual soup served at home!

Ingredients

- 2 tbsp olive oil or sunflower oil
- 25g (approx.1oz) butter
- 1 onion, peeled and chopped
- 1 clove of garlic, peeled and chopped
- ½ tbsp curry paste (curry powder), or to taste
- 500g (approx.1lb 2oz) of parsnips, peeled and chopped
- 1 - 1 ½ litres (approx.1 ¾ - 2 ¾ pts) of vegetable or chicken stock
- Salt and pepper for seasoning

Method

Heat the oil or butter gently in a large saucepan and then add the onion, garlic, curry paste and parsnips. Stir around to coat everything in the oil or butter, and then sweat for 10-15 minutes.

Add the smaller amount of stock (1 litre / 1 ¾ pints) saving the rest for thinning down later if necessary. Season with salt and pepper and bring to the boil, reduce heat and simmer very gently for about 20 minutes until all the vegetables are tender.

Liquidise in batches and return to the pan. Thin with the reserved stock, water or milk as required and check seasoning. Reheat just before eating.

Beef or Chicken Quesadillas

Serves 4

Total cooking time approx 10 minutes

Quesadillas will beat a sandwich any day for hungry students.

Ingredients

- 450g (approx. 1lb) lean beef mince or chopped chicken
- ½ tsp paprika
- 2 pinches cayenne pepper
- 1 tsp sunflower oil
- 8 flour tortillas
- 200g (approx. 7oz) ready made tomato salsa
- 6 spring onions, sliced
- 200g (approx. 7oz) reduced fat Cheddar cheese, grated
- 1 x 20g (approx. 4oz) packet of fresh coriander, chopped
- Sour cream to serve (optional)
- Salt and pepper

Method

Fry the beef or chicken over a high heat until cooked, drain off the fat and stir in the paprika and cayenne pepper. Cook for a further 2-3 minutes and season well with salt and pepper.

In a large frying pan heat the sunflower oil, put in a tortilla and top it with a quarter of the beef or chicken, some salsa, spring onions, cheese and coriander and top it with another tortilla. Press down firmly on the top and allow to heat through for a few seconds.

Using a pallet knife or spatula, turn the filled quesadilla over and cook for a further 2-3 minutes. Repeat the process with the remaining tortillas.

Cut the quesadillas into about 6 wedges and serve with a green salad and some sour cream, if liked.

Creamy Tomato Risotto

Serves 6-8
Total cooking time approx 50 minutes

This is a rich, really yummy dish that for the best results and taste has to be eaten as soon as it is ready.

Ingredients

- 700g (approx. 1 ½ lb) of tomatoes, preferably plum tomatoes
- 1 head of garlic, about 10 cloves
- 350g (approx. 12oz) onions, red onions if available
- 100g (approx. 4 ½ oz) butter
- 30ml (2 level tbsp) sun-dried tomato paste
- 350g (12oz) risotto (Arborio) rice
- 900ml - 1.1 litres (1 ½ - 2 pts) vegetable or chicken stock
- 50 - 75g (approx. 2-3oz) of freshly grated Parmesan cheese
- 3 level tbsp of roughly chopped, fresh flat-leaf parsley
- Salt and freshly ground black pepper
- Deep-fried basil leaves to garnish

Method

De-seed and roughly chop the tomatoes. Place the whole, unpeeled head of garlic in a saucepan and cover with cold water, bring it to the boil and simmer for 15 minutes or until very soft. Remove the garlic from the saucepan, peel and then crush the cloves. Chop the onions.

Heat the butter in a large pan and fry the chopped onions gently, stirring over a medium heat for about 8 minutes or until the onion is soft. Add the tomato paste and cook for 1-2 minutes before adding the crushed garlic and the risotto rice. Fry all the ingredients together for another 1-2 minutes.

Bring the stock to the boil and add a little at a time to the rice mixture, adding more stock when it has been absorbed by the rice. Continue this process until the rice is cooked (about 35 minutes).

When the rice has cooked fully, stir in the chopped tomatoes, grated Parmesan cheese and the parsley. Season the risotto to taste, garnish with the deep-fried basil leaves and serve.

Baked Potatoes
with Bacon, Avocado and Mozzarella

Serves 4

Total cooking time approx 60 - 75 minutes depending on potatoes

Large potatoes are best for this dish e.g. King Edward, Roosters or British Queens. Choose an avocado that is firm but just ripe. Serve the stuffed baked potatoes with a dressed green salad.

Ingredients

For the filling you need

- 100g (approx. 4oz) of streaky bacon snipped into small pieces or bacon lardons
- A little butter or milk
- 1 avocado
- 75g (approx. 3oz) of grated mozzarella or cheddar cheese
- A little paprika
- Salt and freshly ground black pepper

You also need
- *4 large main crop potatoes*

Method

Preheat the oven to 220C / 200C fan-oven / Gas mark 7.

Bake the scrubbed potatoes in the preheated oven for about 1 ¼ hours until cooked through and crisp. If you are short of time cut the potatoes in half before baking, this will reduce cooking time to about 45 minutes.

While the potatoes are cooking, fry the bacon pieces in a non-stick pan until crisp and brown then drain well.

When cooked, remove the potatoes from the oven and leave to cool. Cut the cooled potatoes in half and scoop the potato flesh into a bowl, take care to keep the shells intact. Mash the potato flesh until smooth with a little hot milk and butter.

Half the avocado and remove the stone, skin the halves and cut into small pieces about the size of large peas.

Mix the bacon pieces and the chopped avocado into the mashed potato, seasoning with salt and pepper. Spoon the mash mixture back into the potato skin shells and arrange the shells in a buttered roasting tin or dish filled side up.

Sprinkle the paprika and grated cheese over the filled potato shells and place the roasting dish or tin in the oven. Heat the stuffed potatoes in the oven for about 15 minutes until the cheese is golden brown and the potatoes are heated through.

Mushroom and Bacon Pasta

Serves 2-3
Total cooking time approx 15 minutes

This is a very quick and tasty pasta dish that is ready in about 15 minutes.

Ingredients

- 350g (approx. 12oz) linguine
- 1 tbsp olive oil
- 8 rashers of streaky bacon, chopped or bacon lardons
- 250g (approx. 9oz) mushrooms, sliced
- 1 tbsp thyme (optional)
- 150g (approx. 5oz) frozen peas, defrosted
- 75ml (approx. 2 ½ fl oz) cream
- The juice of ½ a lemon
- Parmesan or Grana Padano cheese shavings, to serve

Method

Cook the pasta according to the instructions on the packet. Drain the cooked pasta and toss with half the olive oil and 2 tablespoons of the cooking water, then set aside.

Heat the remaining olive oil in a frying pan and fry the bacon pieces until crisp, add the sliced mushrooms and thyme and fry for a further 2-3 minutes.

Add to the pasta with the peas and warm over a low heat. When warmed through add the cream and lemon juice and warm further. Serve with the cheese shavings and season.

Roast Chicken Legs with Lemon and Garlic

Serves 4

Total cooking time approx 45 minutes

This is a very simple dish that can be put together by teenagers or students who have been left to fend for themselves.

Ingredients

- 6 tbsp extra virgin olive oil
- 3 large potatoes
- 2 sprigs of fresh rosemary
- 6 cloves of garlic
- 4 chicken quarters
- 2 lemons, sliced
- Salt and freshly ground black pepper

Method

Preheat the oven to 200C / 180C fan-oven / Gas mark 4.

Pour 4 tablespoons of the oil into a roasting tray and place in the heated oven for about 5 minutes.

Cut the potatoes into 2cm cubes leaving the skin on, place in the heated roasting tray with the rosemary. Roast for about 35-40 minutes until golden; add half of the garlic cloves to the potatoes after 20 minutes.

Meanwhile, place the chicken quarters in another roasting tray and season the skin generously with salt and freshly ground black pepper. Drizzle the remaining olive oil over the chicken, add the rest of the cloves of garlic and scatter the lemon slices over the roasting tray. Roast the chicken for 30-35 minutes.

Drain the oil from the cooked potatoes, season with salt and return to the oven for another 5 minutes to crisp up. Serve the chicken with the potatoes.

Chicken and Broccoli Gratin

Serves 6

Total cooking time approx 40 - 80 minutes depending on chicken type used

This fantastic dish can be prepared ahead of time. It is simply a breeze to make and is definitely an all-round winner.

Ingredients

- 6 chicken breasts or 1 whole chicken
- 1 Spanish onion, peeled and chopped
- 2 carrots, peeled and chopped
- 2 sticks of celery, chopped
- A few sprigs of parsley
- 1 bay leaf
- A few black peppercorns
- 300ml (approx. ½ pint) double cream
- 110g (approx. 4 ½ oz) roux*
- 1 large head of broccoli, divided into florets
- 15g (approx. ½oz) of butter
- 110g (approx. 4 ½ oz) breadcrumbs

For the roux* you need
- 50g (approx. 2oz) of butter
- 50g (approx. 2oz) of plain flour

Method

Place the chicken in a large saucepan with the onion, carrots, celery, parsley, bay leaf, peppercorns, and enough cold water to cover. Bring slowly to the boil, then reduce the heat and simmer until the chicken is cooked – about 1 hour for a whole chicken and 20 minutes for chicken breasts. When the chicken is cooked, remove from the saucepan and leave to cool. When cooled, dice the cooked chicken breasts. If you have used a whole chicken strip the meat from the bones, dice and set aside.

Preheat the oven to 180C / 160C fan-oven / Gas mark 4.

Strain the cooking liquid into a saucepan and boil until the volume of liquid has been reduced to about 600ml (approx. 1 pint). Add the cream, return to the boil and whisk in the roux a little at a time to form a thick sauce.

Blanche the broccoli florets in boiling salted water until just tender, then drain and refresh under cold water. Stir the diced chicken and broccoli into the sauce and season to taste with salt and pepper, pour the mixture into an ovenproof dish.

Melt the butter and mix with the breadcrumbs, spread the breadcrumbs over the chicken mixture and bake in the preheated oven for 20 minutes until golden brown and bubbling.

* Roux is a mixture of equal parts butter and flour; it is used to thicken sauces, gravies, milk etc.

To make the roux simply melt the butter in a pan and gradually add the flour, stirring the mixture as you do so. Cook the mixture over a low heat for 1-2 minutes stirring occasionally. It can be stored in a fridge for up to two weeks or made on the spot as required.

Minted Lamb Meatballs with Spaghetti

Serves 6
Total cooking time approx 25 minutes

A really hearty, filling dish. This is a firm favourite with hungry students.

Ingredients

For the meatballs you'll need

- 450g (approx. 1lb) raw lamb mince
- 5 tablespoons of chopped, fresh mint. If you don't have any fresh mint, use 3 tablespoons of mint sauce from a jar.
- 4 tablespoons of sun-dried tomato paste
- 25g (approx.1oz) Parmesan cheese, grated
- 1 small egg, beaten
- 1 tablespoon olive oil
- 2 cloves of garlic, crushed
- 2.5cm (1in) piece of fresh root ginger, grated
- 150ml (¼ pt) red wine
- 2 x 400g tins of chopped tomatoes
- 1 teaspoon of castor sugar
- Salt and freshly ground black pepper for seasoning

You also need

- 350g (approx.12oz) of dried spaghetti

Method

Put the lamb mince, 3 tablespoons of the mint, 2 tablespoons of the sun-dried tomato paste, the Parmesan cheese and the egg together in a large bowl. Season with salt and pepper and mix using your hands, when mixed shape into approximately 30 small meatballs.

Heat the oil in a pan, add the garlic and ginger and fry for about a minute, then add the wine, tomatoes, sugar and the remaining tomato paste. Bring to the boil and then add the meatballs to the sauce, cover and reduce heat to simmer for about 10 minutes or until the meatballs are cooked through.

Cook the pasta in boiling, salted water for about 10 minutes, then drain and tip into a large serving dish.

Add the remaining mint to the sauce, check the seasoning and pour the sauce and meatballs over the spaghetti. Serve with Greek yoghurt and dressed salad leaves.

Preparing ahead: *Cook the meatballs and sauce in advance, they will keep in the fridge for up to a day. This dish also freezes very well.*

Anne's Tip
If you use a lot of grated Parmesan in your cooking you can grate (not too finely) a larger amount than you need and freeze it in a plastic container for future use. You can use as required, adding straight to a dish without any need to thaw it first.

Berry Crumble Deluxe

Total cooking time approx 45 minutes

Crumbles are always a welcome treat with custard or cream, this is a very versatile recipe that can be used with many different types of filling.

Ingredients

- 2 bunches of rhubarb, chopped
- 175g (approx. 6oz) of raspberries
- 2 cooking apples
- 2 tbsp sugar
- 100g (approx. 4oz) self-raising flour
- 100g (approx. 4oz) plain flour
- 175g (approx. 6oz) butter, cubed and chilled
- 100g (approx. 4oz) caster sugar
- 75g (approx. 3oz) hazelnuts, chopped
- Caster sugar for sprinkling

Method

Preheat oven to 190C / 170C fan-oven / Gas mark 5.

Place a baking sheet into the oven to preheat.

Place the chopped rhubarb into a large bowl; add the raspberries, apples and sugar. Mix well and set aside.

Sift the flours into a large bowl, add the butter and rub in with your fingertips until the mixture resembles large breadcrumbs. Stir in the caster sugar and hazelnuts.

Spoon the fruit mixture into a 2.3 litre (approx. 4pt) shallow oven-proof dish and cover with the crumble mixture.

Place the dish on the preheated baking sheet and bake for about 45 minutes until the topping is golden brown and the fruits are tender.

Sprinkle with the extra caster sugar and serve with freshly whipped cream.

My wonderful dinner parties

Dinner parties are a great way of getting together with family and friends and they offer great flexibility regarding times and menus. They are about relaxing, not about spending all your time in the kitchen. For a very relaxed, stress-free dinner party, decide on a menu well in advance and begin preparations as far ahead as possible. The focus of the dinner should be one big dish made in advance, and let everything else fall into place around it. This approach really reduces the stress on the host as well as giving them plenty of time to spend with their guests.

My Wonderful Dinner Parties

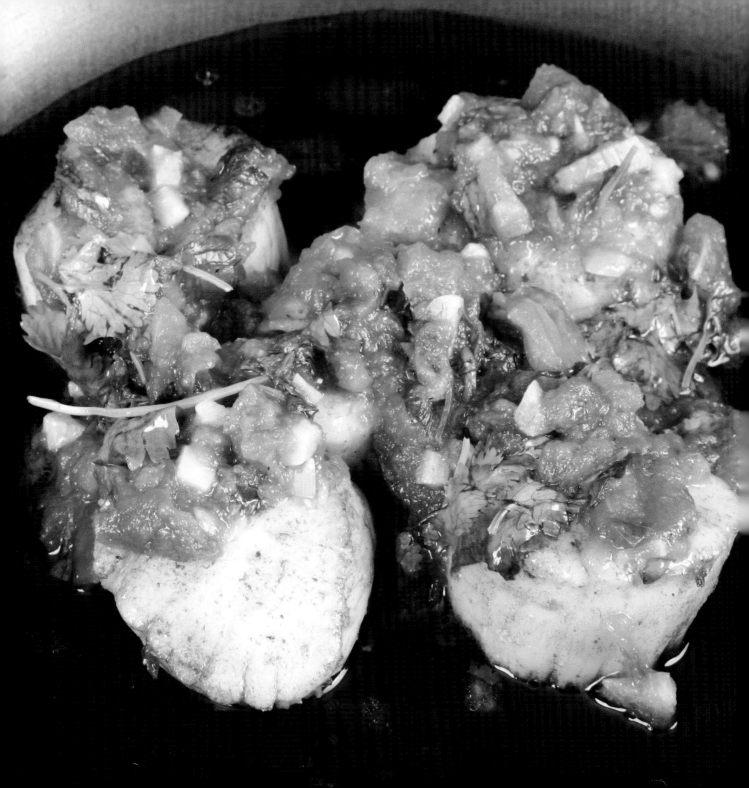

Barbecued Scallops
with Tomatoes and Sauce Vierge

Serves 6 as a starter and 3 as a main course
Total cooking time approx 2 minutes

I love all types of seafood and shellfish but scallops cooked in this way are always the clear winner for me. If you prepare the Sauce vixere beforehand these are great for a picnic cooked on a disposable barbecue.

Ingredients
- 12 large scallops
- Olive oil
- The juice of 1 lemon
- 1 tbsp of chopped coriander
- Salt and freshly ground black pepper

For the Sauce vixere
- 150ml (approx. 4 fl oz) olive oil
- 2 cloves of garlic, finely chopped
- 1 tbsp coriander seeds
- 450g (approx. 1lb) tomatoes, skinned, deseeded and chopped
- 3 tbsp red wine vinegar
- Small handful each of basil, coriander and parsley chopped

Method

Place the scallops in the oil, lemon juice, coriander, salt and pepper and set aside for 1 hour.

For the sauce, warm the olive oil, garlic and coriander seed. Tip in the chopped tomatoes; add the red wine vinegar, the herbs and season with salt and pepper. Keep warm until needed.

Have a large non-stick frying pan good and hot and cook the scallops on both sides for 1 minute. Serve drizzled with the sauce.

Anne's Tip
Do not overcook scallops as this makes them tough, it is better to slightly undercook them if possible. When buying scallop meat that has been removed from the shell avoid meat that is very white or pale in appearance as this has had water added to it to increase the weight. During cooking the water evaporates and the scallops reduce greatly in size and become very tough. Always buy scallops that have a creamy colour.

Baked Mushrooms with Cheese and Pesto

Serves 8 as a starter
Total cooking time approx 20 minutes

The rich pesto helps balance the tangy ricotta and the earthy mushroom flavours of this very easy-to-make starter. This tantalising, unusual starter more than repays the time taken to prepare it.

Ingredients

- 5 tbsp extra virgin olive oil
- 16 medium sized mushrooms
- 250g (approx. 9oz) tub of ricotta or cream cheese
- 3 tbsp green pesto
- 3 cloves of garlic, finely chopped
- 75g (approx. 3oz) of freshly grated Parmesan cheese
- 1 rounded tbsp of pesto and 2 tbsp of chopped, fresh parsley (preferably flatleaf) to serve

Method

Preheat the oven to 200C / 180C fan-oven / Gas mark 6.

If necessary, trim the mushroom stalks level with the caps, then place the mushrooms (rounded cap side down) in the oiled dish. Mix the ricotta or cream cheese with the pesto and garlic and spoon the mixture into the mushrooms (there is enough of the mixture to pile it quite high). Sprinkle the Parmesan cheese over the mushrooms and drizzle over the rest of the olive oil.

Bake the mushrooms in the preheated oven for about 20 minutes or until the mushrooms are soft all the way through and the cheese has just started to turn a golden colour. If this does not happen place the dish under a preheated grill for a few minutes. Sometimes the mushrooms can give off quite a lot of juice during baking, if this has happened you can drain some of it off.

To serve, place the mushrooms on a bed of lettuce leaves and top each mushroom with a small amount of pesto, scatter with the chopped parsley. This dish should be served hot, or at room temperature.

Asparagus Spears
with Free Range Poached Egg and Tarragon Butter

Serves 4
Total cooking time approx 10 minutes

I love the summer months, especially when the asparagus is at its best. There is nothing better for a light lunch than fresh asparagus combined with some of my own free range eggs. This dish takes only 5 minutes to prepare and 10 minutes to cook; perfect for allowing you to make the most of one of our rare sunny days. It is also a life-saver on those occasions when unexpected visitors drop in at lunch time.

Ingredients

- 24 asparagus spears, trimmed
- Salt, to taste
- 1 tbsp of white wine vinegar
- 4 eggs, free range if possible
- 100g (approx. 4oz) butter
- The juice of two lemons
- 2 tbsp of chopped fresh tarragon
- 4 slices of brioche or batch loaf, toasted

Method

Stream the asparagus over plenty of boiling water for 3 to 5 minutes, depending on the thickness of the spears.

Bring a saucepan of salted water to the boil and add the white wine vinegar. Whisk the boiling water to create a whirlpool, when the whirlpool has settled crack an egg into the middle and simmer for 2-3 minutes. Remove the poached egg when cooked to your liking and keep warm. Repeat the operation with the other eggs.

While poaching the eggs melt the butter in a pan and stir in the lemon juice and tarragon. Divide the asparagus spears into four portions and pile each portion onto a slice of toast. Top the piles of asparagus with a poached egg, spoon on the butter sauce and serve immediately.

Thai Fish Cakes with Chilli Dipping Sauce

Serves 4 as a main course - serves 12 as a starter
Total cooking time approx 4 minutes

The freshness of the lemongrass and the heat of the chillies make these little fish cakes a must. Serve them with style by placing cooked fish cakes between the jaws of take-away chopsticks. Just ease the jaws open and gently push a fish cake inside, take care not to break the chopsticks. Serve on a bed of rocket.

Ingredients

For the fish cakes

- 2 shallots, roughly chopped
- 15g coriander, stalks removed
- 4 cloves of garlic, crushed
- 1 stem of lemon grass, peeled and sliced into thin rings
- 3 Kaffir lime leaves, crushed
- 1 cm (approx. ½ in) piece of root ginger, peeled and roughly chopped
- 1-2 small bird's eye chillies, de-seeded and finely chopped
- 1-2 tbsp Thai fish sauce
- 1 small egg, beaten
- 750g (approx. 1lb 11oz) white fish, skinned, boned and cut into chunks
- Salt and freshly ground black pepper
- A little flour
- Ground nut oil for frying

For the chilli dipping sauce

- 1 cup of sugar
- 1 cup of white wine vinegar
- 1 red chilli, de-seeded and finely chopped

Method

Place the prepared shallots, garlic, lime leaves, ginger, chillies and coriander into the bowl of a food processor. Blend together finely. Add the fish and process again until a rough paste is formed, be careful not to over-process.

Scrape the fish mixture into a bowl and stir in the beaten egg and fish sauce, season well.

Shape the mixture into 12 round, flat cakes about 5cm (2in) in diameter, dust your hands with a little flour when handling the fish cakes to prevent them sticking to you. Lay the fish cakes on a tray lined with foil and dust with some flour, cover them with clingfilm and refrigerate while making the chilli dipping sauce.

To make the chilli dipping sauce simply place all the ingredients into a pot, bring to the boil, reduce the heat and simmer until the volume of liquid has been reduced by half.

To cook the fish cakes, heat some sunflower in a non-stick pan, when good and hot place the fish cakes on the pan and cook on one side for 3-4 minutes until crisp. Turn and cook on the other side. When cooked, remove the crisp fish cakes from pan onto some kitchen paper.

Serve on a bed of rocket drizzled with the chilli sauce.

Tomato, Cheese and Black Olive Bread

Makes 1 large loaf
Total cooking time approx 50 minutes

This is just one of many types of homemade bread baked at Ryeland House; it's both delicious and provides a talking point at dinner parties. It is a very versatile recipe; the basic bread mix can form the basis of many interesting variations; try substituting roast vegetables for the tomato and olive elements to create a new treat.

Ingredients

- 250g (approx. 9oz) self-raising flour
- 1 teaspoon of baking powder
- 4 eggs
- 2 tablespoons of olive oil
- 1 tablespoon of white wine
- 2 tablespoons tomato puree
- 150g (approx. 5oz) grated cheddar cheese
- 75g (approx. 3oz) pitted black olives, chopped
- 6 sun-dried tomatoes, chopped
- 3 teaspoons of chopped, mixed fresh herbs

Method

Preheat the oven to 200C / 180C fan-oven / Gas mark 6.

Sieve the flour and baking powder into a bowl and mix in the eggs. Add the olive oil, wine, tomato puree and enough warm water to make a sloppy dough and mix again. Finally, stir in the cheese, olives, sun-dried tomatoes, herbs and some salt and pepper.

Pour the mixture into a greased and lined 450g (approx. 1lb) loaf tin and bake for 30 minutes in the preheated oven.

Reduce the heat to 190C / 170C fan-oven / Gas mark 5 and bake for a further 20 minutes until the loaf is well browned.

To test how well baked the loaf is, turn it out of the tin and tap the bottom of it, a well baked loaf will sound hollow when done. Leave the loaf on a wire rack to cool.

Anne's Tip
This bread can also be made using roasted vegetables such as peppers in place of the sun-dried tomatoes.

Roast Beef
with Tomato and Basil Sauce

Serves 4
Total cooking time approx 35 minutes

Fillet of beef is for those occasions when you have guests that you want to impress; it certainly has the wow factor!

Ingredients

- 800g (approx. 1lb 12oz) beef fillet
- 2 tbsp of olive oil
- 1 red onion, finely sliced
- 300g (approx. 11oz) of cherry tomatoes, halved
- 1 tbsp red wine vinegar
- 100ml (approx. 3 ½ fl oz) of hot beef or vegetable stock
- A small handful of basil leaves, roughly torn

Method

Preheat the oven to 200C / 180C fan-oven / Gas mark 6.

Season the fillet of beef with salt and freshly ground black pepper. Heat 1 tablespoon of olive oil in a large frying pan and fry the beef for 5 minutes, turning until brown on all sides. Place the beef in a warmed roasting tin and roast for 20-30 minutes; the beef should still be pink in the middle.

While the beef is roasting add the remaining oil to the pan in which you fried the beef. Add the red onion and cook for 5-10 minutes over a medium heat until softened and golden. Place the cherry tomatoes into the pan and cook for 5 minutes until they have begun to soften.

Pour in the vinegar and stock and bring to the boil, allow it to bubble for 1-2 minutes then add the basil. Taste and adjust the seasoning if necessary, keep the sauce warm until serving.

When the beef has been roasted enough, remove from the oven and cover it with kitchen foil, allow the meat to rest for about 10 minutes. Slice the beef and serve with the tomato and basil sauce, fresh Irish asparagus (when in season). Some new potatoes will compliment the beef perfectly.

Tagine of Lamb with Prunes and Ras el Hanout

Serves 4
Total cooking time approx 2 hours 15 minutes

Spices lose their pungency with age, so it is best to blend the Ras El Hanout only as required. This blend of spices can also be used with cod, salmon, haddock or monkfish; it is also very good with chicken. The fish or chicken can be rolled in the spices and fried in pure olive oil. This recipe makes about 3 tablespoons of Ras El Hanout.

Ingredients

For the Tagine of Lamb

- 1 kg boneless lamb shoulder steaks
- ¼ cup olive oil
- 1 onion, chopped
- 4 cloves of garlic, chopped
- 2 tbsp freshly grated ginger
- 1 tbsp Ras el Hanout spice blend
- ¼ cup chopped coriander, plus an extra 2 tbsp to serve
- ¼ cup of liquid honey
- ½ tsp saffron threads dissolved in ½ cup of boiling water
- 1 ½ cups of beef stock
- 1 ½ cups of pitted prunes
- Sea salt and freshly ground black pepper
- 2 tbsp of toasted sesame seeds

Method

Trim the skin and excess fat from the lamb and cut into 4cm pieces. Heat a large pan; add half the oil and brown the cubed lamb on both sides (this may need to be done in 2 or 3 batches). Remove the browned lamb pieces from the pan and reserve.

Add the onion, garlic and ginger to the pan with the remaining olive oil and cook over a medium heat for 5 minutes, stirring constantly. The Ras el Handout spice mix is now added to the pan and cooked for 1 minute to toast the spices and release the flavours.

Return the browned lamb pieces to the pan and add the coriander, honey, saffron liquid and the stock. Half cover the pan with a lid and bring the liquid to a boil, reduce the heat and simmer for 1 hour, turning the lamb pieces occasionally.

Add the prunes and cook for another 45 minutes until the lamb and prunes are tender and the liquid is much reduced. Alternatively, the cooking can be done in an oven preheated to 180C.

Skim any excess fat from the surface of the dish and adjust the seasoning of the sauce to taste. Sprinkle with sesame seeds and extra coriander to serve. Serve with couscous.

Ras el Hanout

Ingredients

For the Ras el Hanout

- 1 tsp each of coriander, fennel and cumin seeds, toasted and ground
- 1 tsp ground turmeric
- 1 tsp ground paprika
- 1 tsp ground cinnamon
- ½ tsp cayenne pepper
- ½ tsp ground nutmeg
- ½ tsp ground all spice
- ½ tsp ground cardamom
- ½ tsp sea salt
- ½ tsp freshly ground black pepper

Method

Simply combine all the spices and store in an airtight container.

Chocolate Rum and Raisin Torte

Serves 8-10

Total cooking time approx 40 minutes

My son is a complete chocoholic and this is his all-time favourite. It is simply delicious, a very indulgent treat for chocolate lovers.

Ingredients

For the torte

- 75g (approx. 3oz) raisins
- 75ml (approx. 2 ½ fl oz) dark rum
- 100g (approx. 4oz) of butter, cubed plus extra for greasing
- 200g (approx. 8oz) plain chocolate, broken into pieces
- 4 eggs free-range if possible, separated
- 100g (approx. 4oz) caster sugar
- 55g (approx. 2oz) plain flour
- 85g (approx. 3oz) ground almonds

For the topping

- 250g (approx. 9oz) plain chocolate, broken into pieces
- 200ml (approx. 7 fl oz) of double cream
- 3 tbsp of dark rum
- Strawberries, for decoration
- 1 tsp cocoa powder, for dusting

Method

Place the raisins in a bowl; pour the rum over them and leave to soak overnight.

Preheat the oven to 200C / 180C fan-oven / Gas mark 6. Grease and line the base of a 20cm (8in) round, loose-bottom cake tin with parchment

Place the chocolate in a bowl, set to melt over a saucepan of simmering water and stir gently until smooth. Gradually stir in the butter until melted then remove from the heat.

Beat the egg yolks and sugar until pale, then stir in the chocolate. Sift the flour over the chocolate mix; fold in along with the almonds and the rum-soaked raisins.

Whisk the egg whites until stiff and fold in the chocolate mix, pour into the prepared cake tin and bake for 35-40 minutes. Leave the cake to cool for about 10 minutes and then remove it from the tin.

While the cake is in the oven, prepare the topping. Place the chocolate pieces in a large bowl. Heat the rum and cream together in a saucepan until just boiling, pour over the chocolate and stir until melted and smooth. Cool the mixture for 5 minutes, stirring occasionally to achieve a good icing consistency. Spread the chocolate icing over the top and sides of the torte, then decorate with strawberries and dust with the cocoa powder.

Ginger Crème Brulee and Plum Compote

Serves 6

Total cooking time approx 60 minutes

This dish is very versatile and has many possible variations, instead of ginger you can use vanilla, orange or rhubarb. Frozen mixed berries can be substituted for the raspberries or blackberries. This is a great dish to experiment with so why not try out some of your own ideas.

Ingredients

For the brulee

- 600ml (approx. 1 pt) of cream
- 6 tbsp of finely chopped ginger
- 6 egg yolks
- 6 tsp caster sugar
- 6 ramekins

For the compote

- 2 tbsp unsalted butter
- 3 ripe plums, pitted and sliced
- 2-3 tbsp of caster sugar (depending on the ripeness of the fruit)
- 60ml (approx. 2 fl oz) orange juice
- 250g (approx. 9oz) fresh raspberries or blackberries
- 100g (approx. 4oz) light brown sugar passed through a sieve

Method

Preheat the oven to 165C / 150C fan-oven / Gas mark 3.

In a saucepan bring the cream and ginger to a simmer over a medium heat, reduce the heat to low and simmer for 30 minutes. Strain the cream and discard the ginger.

In a bowl, whisk the egg yolks and sugar together until very well combined and the mixture is pale yellow. Gradually add the cream to the egg mixture, skimming off any foam.

Place the ramekins into a large baking pan. Pour the brulee mixture into the dishes and place the baking pan in the centre of the oven. Pour enough hot water into the baking pan to come halfway up the sides of the ramekins. Bake for about 30 minutes or until the custards are just set, remove from the oven and allow them to cool. Chill until ready to use.

Heat the butter in a saucepan and then add the fruit and sugar, cook together for 3-4 minutes. Add the orange juice to the pan and cook over a medium heat for about 2 minutes until the mixture is slightly thickened. At this stage add the berries and remove the saucepan from the heat, keep the compote warm until ready to serve.

To finish, sprinkle the sugar over the top of the custards and carefully cook under a hot grill until the sugar has caramelised. Serve with the compote.

Anne's Tip

Different versions of this dish can be made by simply substituting another ingredient for the finely chopped ginger. Some of the successful variations I have used are, • Vanilla - use 2-3 tsp of pure vanilla extracts • Orange - use the finely grated rind of 2 oranges • Rhubarb - use 2-3 sticks

Lemon Almond Biscuits

Makes about 36 individual biscuits or 18 filled
Approx cooking time 15 minutes

These are simple but deliciously crumbly; they can be enjoyed individually or carefully sandwiched together with a citrus butter-cream filling. Either way they make an elegant and delicate treat.

Ingredients

For the biscuits you need

- The grated zest of 1 lemon
- 125g (approx. 4 ½oz) of golden caster sugar
- 2 large egg yolks
- 250g (approx. 9oz) of plain flour
- 50g (2 oz) ground almonds
- 130g (approx. 5oz) unsalted butter

For the citrus butter-cream (optional)

- The grated zest of 1 small lemon
- The grated zest of 1 orange
- 125g (approx. 4 ½oz) unsalted butter, at room temperature
- 125g (approx. 4 ½oz) golden caster sugar

Method

Preheat the oven to 180C / 160C fan-oven / Gas mark 4.

Put the butter and sugar into the bowl of a food mixer and beat until light and creamy. Beat in the egg yolks and the lemon zest, the mixture may curdle slightly at this point but don't worry. Add the ground almonds and flour and mix briefly, just until the mixture comes together.

Take small lumps of the dough (about the size of a walnut in its shell), and roll them into ball shapes between the palms of your hands. Put them on 2 greased baking sheets (they shouldn't spread too much), using the back of the prongs of a fork, press down on each one so that they flatten slightly.

Bake the biscuits for about 12-15 minutes in the preheated oven; swap the positions of the baking sheets half way through the baking process to ensure even baking. When the biscuits are slightly coloured but not golden brown, remove the sheets from the oven. Allow the biscuits to cool briefly then transfer to cooling racks using a palette knife.

If you opt to make the butter-cream beat the butter and sugar together in a bowl until soft and fluffy, add the grated citrus zest and continue beating until well mixed. Carefully sandwich the biscuits together with the butter-cream filling.

Alma's Favourite Apple Tart

Serves 10
Total cooking time approx 50 minutes

Alma has worked with me here in Ryeland House for a number of years and she says that of all the dishes she has helped to prepare, and later eaten, this is her absolute favourite.

Ingredients

For the pastry

- 100g (approx. 4oz) chilled butter, cubed
- 225g (approx. 8oz) plain white flour
- 25g (approx. 1oz) icing sugar, sifted
- 1 egg beaten

For the filling

- 4 eggs
- 225g (approx. 8oz) caster sugar
- The grated zest and juice of 2 lemons
- 100g (approx. 4oz) butter, melted
- 5 large cooking apples, peeled, cored and quartered
- 2 dessert apples, peeled, cored, quartered and thinly sliced
- 25g (approx. 1oz) Demerara sugar

Method

Preheat the oven to 200C / 180C fan-oven / Gas mark 6. Grease a 23cm (9in) loose-bottom tart tin.

If making the pastry by hand, rub the butter into the flour and icing sugar until the mixture resembles breadcrumbs. Then stir in the beaten egg and bring together to form a dough.

If making the pastry in a food processor, combine the butter, flour and icing sugar in the bowl of the processor and process until the mixture resembles ground almonds. Pour in the beaten egg and pulse until the mixture forms a ball of dough around the central stem.

Regardless of the method used to make the pastry, form the pastry into a smooth ball, place in a plastic bag and chill for 30 minutes.

Roll out the pastry on a lightly floured surface, slightly larger than the tin. Use a rolling pin to lift the pastry into the tin, trim the edges and prick all over the base using a fork. Place the pastry lined tin in the fridge to chill for 30 minutes.

While the pastry is chilling put a heavy metal baking tray in the oven to heat. Beat the eggs, sugar, lemon zest and juice in a large bowl. Stir in the warm, melted butter then coarsely grate the cooking apples directly into the mixture and mix well.

Remove the chilled pastry casing from the fridge and spread the lemon mixture in the base. Level the surface of the filling using the back of a spoon and arrange the dessert apple slices around the outside edge, neatly overlapping. Sprinkle the slices with Demerara sugar.

Place the tart on the warmed baking tray and bake for 45-50 minutes, or until the centre of the tart feels firm to the touch and the apple slices are tinged with brown. Serve the tart warm with cream.

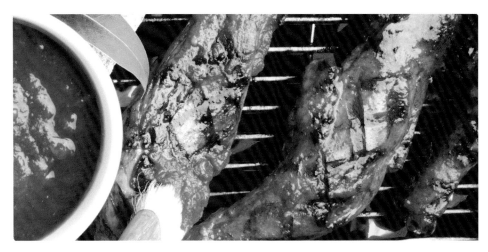

Summer Salads and Barbecuing

Summers in Ireland are always a bit hit and miss when it comes to the weather. If there is even the remotest chance of a dry, sunny day, pull out the barbecue. Tasty food cooked in the open is one of the great, simple pleasures in life and should be enjoyed whenever possible. When my children were young they liked nothing better than a barbecue on the beach and simple food has never tasted so good, even those "very well cooked" burgers and sausages.

Summer is the season for salads and barbecues; it's also a great opportunity to experiment with new tastes, especially for marinades and salad dressings.

Summer Salads and Barbecuing

Marinades and Salad Dressings

Great Marinade Recipes

The amount of time needed to marinate fish is about 30 minutes and meats need approximately 1 hour (but knowing our Irish weather you might only have 20 minutes!).

Classic BBQ

In a small saucepan put 2 tbsp of red wine vinegar, 5 tbsp of tomato sauce, 1 tbsp Dijon mustard, a dash of Worcestershire sauce, 1 tsp chilli powder and 3 tbsp brown sugar. Bring the contents of the pan to the boil, reduce heat and simmer for 2 minutes.

Good for pork, ribs and sausages.

Thai Sweet Chilli

Finely chop the following ingredients, a thumb sized piece of ginger, 2 red chillies, 1 stick of lemon grass and a clove of garlic. Mix the chopped ingredients with the juice of 1 lime, 1 tbsp of fish sauce, 1 tbsp of groundnut oil and 2 tbsp of caster sugar.

Good for beef and fish.

Satay

Put 3 tbsp of smooth peanut butter, 2 tbsp of soy sauce and 2 tbsp of sweet chilli sauce in a small saucepan with 4 tbsp of water and 2 tbsp of coconut milk. Heat gently, whisking the ingredients together until smooth.

Good for chicken.

Moroccan

Simply mix 4 tbsp of harissa with the juice of 2 lemons and 3 tbsp of olive oil.

Good for lamb and fish.

Chinese 5 Spice

Mix 1 tbsp of Chinese 5 Spice with 4 tbsp of soy sauce, 2 tsp sesame oil and 2 tbsp of ground nut oil.

Good for chicken and pork.

Citrus and Herb

Roughly chop a small bunch of both parsley and basil. Mix the chopped herbs with the juice of 1 lemon, the juice of 1 orange and 3 tbsp of olive oil. Season the mixture well with salt and freshly ground black pepper.

Good for fish and chicken.

Tandoori

Mix together 300ml of natural yoghurt, 3 tbsp of Tandoori mix, 1 tsp of chilli powder, the juice of 1 lemon, 2 tbsp of olive oil and 1 crushed clove of garlic.

Good for fish, chicken and lamb.

Honey Mustard

Mix 2 tbsp of Dijon mustard with 2 tbsp of runny honey, the juice of 1 orange and 2 tbsp of sunflower oil.

Good for pork.

Hot Sweet and Smoked

Mix 1 tsp of smoked paprika with 1 tsp of chilli powder, 1 grated red onion, 1 tbsp of honey and the juice of 1 lemon.

Good for lamb.

Sweet and Sour Cucumber Dip

Serves 6-8 as part of a salad

Ingredients

- 2 cups of cucumber, quartered and thinly sliced
- 4 tbsp of sugar
- 2 tbsp of shallots, finely chopped
- 1 tbsp of red chilli, finely cut
- 1 tbsp of salt
- 3 tbsp of rice wine vinegar

Method

Mix together the sugar, salt and rice wine vinegar. Add all the other ingredients and stir well. Refrigerate for at least one hour before serving.

Homemade Pesto

Stir into Pasta or serve as a salad dressing.

Ingredients

- 15g (approx. a good ½ oz) basil
- 1 tbsp of pine nuts
- 1 clove of garlic
- 1 tbsp of freshly grated Parmesan cheese
- 180ml (approx. 6 fl oz) of olive oil

Method

To make the pesto simply place all the ingredients into a blender and blitz until you reach the desired consistency.

Red Pepper Pesto

The Red Pepper Pesto can be added to hot pasta and served with grated Parmesan cheese. It is also brilliant with beef or chicken from the barbecue.

Ingredients

- 3 red peppers - sliced, roasted and skinned
- 2-3 tbsp of fresh basil
- 2 cloves of garlic, crushed
- 50g (approx. 2oz) of Parmesan cheese
- 50g (approx. 2oz) of pine nuts
- 2 anchovy fillets
- The juice of ½ lemon
- 4 tbsp of olive oil

Method

Place all the ingredients into a food processor and whiz together.

Anne's Tip

To make removing the skins from roasted red peppers easier, simply remove the roasted peppers from the oven and immediately place them in a plastic bag or wrap tightly in clingfilm. Roll the pepper slices up in a clean tea towel to keep warm and leave for about 30 minutes, remove the pepper slices from the wrapping and peel off the skins.

Slow Roasted Tomatoes

Total cooking time approx 3 - 4 hours

These tomatoes have a delicious, intense flavour and can be stored in olive oil in screw-top jars for up to a month.

Ingredients

- 1 punnet of cherry/plum tomatoes
- A bunch of mixed herbs e.g. parsley, chives and basil
- Extra virgin olive oil
- Sea salt and freshly ground black pepper

Method

Preheat the oven to 110C / 100C fan-oven / Gas mark ¼

Cut the cherry tomatoes into halves or the plum tomatoes into quarters and place on a greased oven tray cut side up. Sprinkle the mixed herbs over the tomatoes and season with sea salt and freshly ground black pepper.

Place the tray in the oven and roast for approximately 3-4 hours. Allow the tomatoes to cool and then use or store in jars for later.

Barbecue Sauce

Makes about 2 cups

You can store any unused barbecue sauce in a covered container in the fridge.

Ingredients

- 2 onions, sliced
- 2 cloves of garlic, crushed
- 2 tbsp of sunflower oil
- ¼ cup of red wine vinegar
- ¼ cup of brown sugar
- 2 tbsp of grainy mustard
- 1 tbsp of Worcestershire sauce
- 400g tin of chopped tomatoes
- 1 tsp of salt
- 2 tbsp of tomato paste

Method

Sauté the onions and garlic in the oil until tender. Stir in the vinegar, sugar, mustard, Worcestershire sauce, the undrained tomatoes, tomato paste and the salt.

Bring the mixture to the boil, reduce the heat and simmer uncovered for about 30 minutes. Puree the sauce in a blender or push the mixture through a sieve. The sauce can be served either hot or cold.

Carrot with Roasted Sesame Seeds

Serves 6-8

Simple and full of colour this combination works so well it deserves to join the ranks of the classics such as Caesar or nicoise. In this dish the carrots' pedigree is vital, choose organic if possible and nothing too old. Crunch and good colour is essential, lacklustre specimens need not apply!
As far as quantities are concerned this salad should be made to taste; as a guide use about 1 dessertspoon of sesame seeds to 4 large carrots. You can also use other seeds such as poppy, pumpkin, linseed or even pine nuts.

Ingredients

- 1 dsp of sesame seeds
- 4 coarsely grated carrots
- French Dressing

For the French dressing
Everyone has their own French dressing. The proportions vary, as do the ingredients, but this is the combination that works best for us. You can use this recipe as a basis and experiment until you find the perfect combination for your taste.

- 150ml (approx. ¼ pt) of sunflower oil
- 150ml (approx. ¼ pt) of olive oil
- 150ml (approx. ¼ pt) of peanut oil
- 150ml (approx. ¼ pt) red wine vinegar
- Salt and freshly ground black pepper
- 1 clove of garlic
- 1 tbsp grainy mustard
- 1 dessertspoon of honey

Method

For the French Dressing
Place all the ingredients in a blender or food processor and liquidise. This can be stored in a bottle and shaken vigorously before use. It will keep in the fridge for several weeks.

For the salad
Roast the sesame seeds in a dry frying pan. Add them to the grated carrot and toss with 3 tbsp of the French dressing. Check the seasoning and serve.

Cherry Tomato, Chive and Basil Frittata

Serves 2
Total cooking time approx 10 minutes

Frittata is just an upmarket version of an omelette, however it is just as quick and easy to make as its less posh cousin.

Ingredients

- 2 cloves of garlic, unpeeled
- 4 tbsp of olive oil
- 1 punnet of cherry tomatoes, slow roasted
- 8 eggs, lightly beaten and seasoned
- 2 tbsp of grated Parmesan cheese
- 2 generous handfuls of basil
- 2 tbsp of finely chopped chives

Method

Heat the olive oil in a small saucepan. Crush the cloves of garlic and poach in the hot olive oil for about 5 minutes or until golden brown then discard the garlic.

Beat the eggs and Parmesan cheese together and then add the infused olive oil, the basil, chives and some salt and pepper.

Lightly oil a non-stick pan, heat the pan and pour in the egg mixture then add in the slow roasted tomatoes. Cook the mixture until set and finish off under a preheated grill.

Greek Island Salad with Chicken and Avocado

Serves 6

This is an excellent dish to prepare ahead of use, a great way to reduce the workload when you have visitors.

Ingredients

- 1.8 kg (approx. 4lb) roasted chicken at room temperature
- 2 hearts of romaine lettuces
- 4 tomatoes
- 2 spring onions
- 2 ripe avocados
- 3 tbsp of lemon juice, plus extra for squeezing
- 200g (approx. 7oz) packet of feta cheese
- ½ tsp dried oregano
- ½ tsp dried mint
- Half a bunch of flatleaf parsley
- 5 tbsp of extra virgin olive oil
- 2 tbsp kalamata olives
- Pitta bread, to serve (optional)

Method

Pull the meat from the chicken and roughly shred.

Trim the base from the lettuces, wash and dry the leaves then roughly shred. Cut the tomatoes into wedges and finely slice the spring onions.

Halve the avocados, remove the stones and peel. Cut the avocado halves crosswise into strips then squeeze a little lemon juice over them.

Crumble the feta cheese and toss with the oregano and mint. Pick the leaves off the parsley and set aside. Whisk the lemon juice with the olive oil and season.

In a large bowl, toss the chicken, lettuce, tomatoes and spring onions, fold through three quarters of the dressing with the avocado slices. Season the salad then scatter over the feta, olives and parsley, drizzle with the rest of the dressing.

Squeeze extra lemon juice on top and serve with pitta bread if you choose.

Trout or Sea Bass with Cucumber and Dipping Sauce

Serves 4
Total cooking time approx 20 minutes

Wild trout or sea bass, like free range chicken, has the best taste and texture but restrictions on fishing to conserve fish stocks often means that the wild varieties are unavailable. However, fish farmers have reacted to consumer demands for better quality products and now good quality farmed fish can make a very acceptable substitute for the wild varieties.

At Ryeland House we are lucky in having a very good trout farm close to us so I can get great quality trout fresh any day I need it.   Very tasty!!!!!

Ingredients

- 4 Trout or sea Bass fillets
- 1 thumb sized red chilli, deseeded and finely chopped
- 2 cloves of garlic, finely chopped
- A handful of coriander, roughly chopped
- 1 tbsp of fish sauce
- 1 tbsp of sesame oil
- 2 tbsp of clear honey
- ¼ cucumber, diced
- ½ a red onion, diced

For the dipping sauce
- 4 tbsp of sweet chilli sauce, mixed with a squeeze of lime juice

Method

In a bowl mix together the chilli, garlic, coriander, fish sauce, sesame oil and honey and season with freshly ground black pepper.   Place the trout or sea bass fillets in the marinade and refrigerate for at least 20 minutes, take care not to over marinate as this will affect the taste of the fish.

Place the marinated fillets on a hot barbecue and cook until they are crisp at the edges. If you like fish cooked all the way through rather than rare in the middle keep cooking the fillets until they feel firm to the touch.

Serve the fillets with the diced cucumber and onion sprinkled over and the sweet chilli dipping sauce.

Roast Tomato and Mozzarella Galette with Basil

Serves 4
Total cooking time approx 13 minutes

This galette can be assembled very easily using pre-made puff pastry.

Ingredients

- 1 sheet (about 200g) of puff pastry, thawed if frozen
- 4 tsp of tapenade or black olive paste
- 6 slow roasted tomatoes or (in the summer) slices of ripe tomatoes
- 2 buffalo mozzarella, sliced
- 2 handfuls of fresh basil
- 12 semi sun-dried tomatoes, roughly chopped

Method

Preheat the oven to 200C / 180C fan-oven / Gas mark 6.

Line a shallow baking tray with baking paper. Roll out the puff pastry and cut into four discs using a 10cm pastry cutter. Prick the pastry discs well with a fork and place on the prepared baking tray.

Cover the pastry with another sheet of baking paper/parchment and weigh it down with a second baking tray. Bake in the preheated oven for 10-15 minutes. The two baking trays help keep the pastry rounds in a circular shape, otherwise they tend to become ovals.

Spread the tapenade or black olive paste on each pastry disc. Arrange the slow-roasted tomatoes on top and cover with the sliced mozzarella.

Return the pastry rounds to the oven for a few minutes until the cheese starts to melt. Decorate by scattering the basil and chopped semi sun-dried tomatoes on top of the melted cheese.

Barbecued Coriander Lamb

Serves 6
Total cooking time approx 1 ½ hours

You need a barbecue with a lid for this recipe. Light one side of the barbecue only, leaving the other off. Place the meat on the off side of the barbecue and close the lid, this circulates the heat within the barbecue and the meat is cooked using the indirect heat. This cooking method results in wonderfully tender meat that almost melts in your mouth.

Ingredients

- 1 tbsp coriander seeds
- 1 tbsp cumin
- A large bunch of fresh coriander, chopped
- The juice of 1 lemon
- Extra virgin olive oil
- 3 cloves of garlic, crushed
- 1 tub of Greek yoghurt
- 1.6kg (approx. 3 ½ lb) leg of lamb, boned and butterflied (ask your butcher to do this for you)

Method

Heat the barbecue.

Put the coriander and cumin seeds in a pestle and mortar and crush slightly. Mix together the chopped coriander, yoghurt, lemon juice, 2 tbsp of olive oil, crushed garlic and crushed spices.

Smear the mixture all over the lamb and marinate for at least and hour. Season well and cook on the barbecue as described above for about 1 ½ hours with the lid closed. Turn the lamb a few times during the cooking process.

When the lamb has cooked to your liking remove it from the barbecue and rest it for about 10 minutes, slice and serve.

Anne's Tip
If you don't have a fancy barbecue don't panic, this recipe works very well with a fan oven. Follow the directions for marinating the lamb and then cook the lamb in a fan oven, preheated to 180C, for about 1 ¼ hours for medium and about 1 ¾ hours for well done.

Summer Barbecue Chicken

Serves 4
Total cooking time approx 30 minutes

The men who attend my classes absolutely love this dish for its simplicity and taste.

Ingredients

- 4 chicken fillets
- 2 tbsp tomato sauce
- 1 tbsp soy sauce
- 2 tbsp balsamic vinegar
- 50g (approx. 2oz) of brown sugar
- 1 tsp of wholegrain mustard
- 1 orange, rind and juice
- 1 tbsp Golden Syrup
- 1 tbsp tomato puree
- 1 tbsp of chopped parsley, for garnish
- Salt and freshly ground black pepper

Method

Mix all the ingredients, except for the chicken fillets and garnish, in a large bowl and season. Place the chicken fillets into the marinade and ensure that they are well coated with the marinade. Cover the bowl and leave for at least 3 hours, or better still, leave overnight in the fridge.

When the chicken fillets have marinated, preheat the oven to 190C / 170C fan-oven / Gas mark 5.

Place the marinated fillets onto a baking tray and cook for 25-30 minutes. Serve the fillets piled high on a plate and garnish them with some of the chopped parsley.

Anne's Tip
The fillets can also be cooked on a barbecue and taste fantastic this way. To cook the chicken using a barbecue wait until the fillets have marinated for a sufficient amount of time. Place the marinated chicken fillets on a hot barbecue and cook for about 10 minutes on each side. Make sure that the chicken is well cooked before serving.

Sizzling Asian Steak with Dipping Sauce

Serves 4
Total cooking time approx 4 minutes

This is a Malaysian method of sizzling meat on a hot barbecue.

Ingredients

For the steaks

- 4 x 200g (approx. 7oz) sirloin steaks
- 1 clove of garlic, crushed
- 2.5cm (approx. 1in) piece of fresh ginger, finely chopped
- 2 tsp of black pepper corns
- 1 tbsp of sugar
- 2 tbsp tamarind sauce
- 3 tbsp dark soy sauce
- 1 tbsp oyster sauce
- Vegetable oil for brushing
- Carrots and spring onion, shredded to garnish

For the Dipping Sauce

- 5 tbsp of beef stock
- 2 tbsp of tomato ketchup
- 1 tsp of chilli sauce
- The juice of 1 lime

Method

Place the steaks in a single layer in a shallow dish. Pound together the garlic, ginger, peppercorns and sugar using a mortar and pestle. When the spices are pounded add in the tamarind sauce, soy sauce and the oyster sauce and mix together to make the marinade. Spoon the marinade over the layer of steaks, turning the steaks to coat evenly. Set the dish aside to marinate the steaks for up to eight hours.

When the steaks have marinated to your taste, scrape the marinade off each side of the steaks into a saucepan. Add the beef stock, tomato ketchup, chilli sauce and limejuice and simmer briefly. Keep the dipping sauce warm on the side of the barbecue.

Brush the steaks with vegetable oil and cook on the barbecue for about 2 minutes on each side, or according to taste. Garnish the steaks with shredded carrot and spring onion. Serve with the warm dipping sauce.

Chicken Satay

Serves 6
Total cooking time approx 10 minutes

This is always a popular addition to any barbecue menu and it adds a little variety to the proceedings.

Ingredients

For the chicken

- 6 chicken breasts
- 4 tbsp of light soy sauce
- 2 tsp of salt
- 8 tbsp of oil
- 3 tbsp curry powder
- 240ml (approx. 8 fl oz) coconut milk
- 18 x 15cm (approx. 6in) satay sticks

For the sauce

- 2 tbsp of oil
- 3 cloves of garlic, finely chopped
- 1 tbsp of red curry paste or hot curry paste
- 120ml (approx. 4 fl oz) of coconut milk
- 250ml (approx. 8 fl oz) stock broth
- 1tbsp brown sugar
- 1 tsp of salt
- 1 tbsp of lemon juice
- 4 tbsp smooth peanut butter

Method

Cut the chicken breasts into fine slices. In a bowl mix together the soy sauce, salt, curry powder, oil, 240ml of coconut milk and the sugar. Place the sliced chicken breasts in the marinade, make sure all the slices are coated and stand for 6 hours or overnight if preferred.

To make the sauce, heat some oil in a pan until very hot and slightly smoking. Add the chopped garlic and fry until brown then put in the curry powder, stir and cook for about 10 seconds.

Pour in coconut milk, stock, salt, sugar, and the lemon juice, blend the ingredients well together and cook for 3 minutes, stirring all the time. Finally, add the peanut butter and mix thoroughly.

Thread the marinated chicken slices onto the satay sticks. Using a hot pan full of sunflower oil or a hot barbecue cook the chicken for about 7 minutes or until the chicken is completely cooked.

Coat the cooked chicken with the peanut sauce and garnish with a red chilli and a sprig of coriander. Serve with sweet and sour cucumber dip if desired.

Anne's Tip
Soak the wooden skewers for 20 or 30 minutes before use to prevent them from burning during cooking.

Smoked Bacon, Blue Cheese and Pineapple Pasta

Serves 6
Total cooking time approx 15 minutes

This pasta dish makes a great main course and can be adapted for your vegetarian friends by simply substituting tofu for the bacon.

Ingredients

- 500g (approx. 18oz) penne
- 225g (approx. 8oz) of smoked bacon
- 110g (approx. 4 ½ oz) of mangetout, cut into narrow strips
- 50g (approx. 2oz) baby spinach leaves, shredded
- 200g (approx. 7oz) can of pineapple
- 50g (approx. 2oz) of flaked almonds, toasted plus a few extra to garnish
- 110g (approx. 4 ½ oz) of Cashel Blue or other blue cheese, crumbled
- 110g (approx. 4 ½ oz) Greek style yoghurt
- 110g (approx. 4 ½ oz) of mayonnaise
- Chopped fresh chives, to garnish

Method

Cook the pasta in plenty of salted water until tender, then drain and set aside.

Cut the bacon into bite-sized pieces and fry in a dry frying pan until they are very crisp, drain the bacon pieces on kitchen towel and set aside.

Place the cooked pasta, fried bacon, spinach, pineapple pieces (reserving the juice) and almonds in a large bowl.

To make the dressing, blend together the blue cheese, yoghurt, mayonnaise and the juice from the canned pineapple.

Toss the pasta and the other ingredients with the dressing and adjust the seasoning; be cautious with the salt as the bacon may be salty enough.

To serve, garnish with some chopped chives and a few toasted flaked almonds.

Summer Scones with Strawberries

Makes approx 12 scones
Total cooking time approx 18-20 minutes

Ingredients

For the scones

- 450g (approx. 1lb) self raising flour
- 1 tsp baking powder
- 125g (approx. 5oz) unsalted butter
- 100g (approx. 4oz) of sugar
- 2 eggs
- 225ml (approx. 7fl oz) milk

For the filling

- Whipped cream mixed with rose water and strawberries or strawberry jam

Method

Preheat the oven to 220C / 200C fan-oven / Gas mark 7.

Sieve the flour into a bowl and add the baking powder.

Rub in the butter and add the sugar.

Mix the milk and eggs together and add to the dry mixture to make a soft dough.

Turn the dough out onto a floured board and knead lightly.

Roll out the dough and cut into approximately 14 circles, place the circles on a greased baking tray. Brush the circles with an egg wash and bake in the preheated oven for about 20 minutes.

Cool on a wire rack when cooked and serve with cream and strawberries or cream and strawberry jam.

Homemade Strawberry Jam

This homemade jam really compliments the homemade scones, especially when served with fresh, whipped cream.

Ingredients

- 900g (approx. 2lb) strawberries
- 900g (approx. 2lb) of sugar (warmed in the oven)
- The juice of 1 large lemon

Anne's Tip

To test your jam for setting, place a saucer in the fridge and allow the saucer to become good and cold. Place a tablespoon of jam onto the cold saucer and return to the fridge. After 5 minutes push the jam with your finger, if the surface of the jam wrinkles the jam is set.

Method

Preheat the oven to 160C / 145C fan-oven / Gas mark 3.

Crush the fruit slightly and place the sugar in the oven to warm.

Put the crushed fruit into a large stainless steel saucepan and add 2 tbsp of cold water and the lemon juice. Heat the fruit slowly until the juices begin to flow.

Add the warmed sugar and stir until the sugar has dissolved then boil rapidly and test for setting. If the jam does not set, boil for another 2 minutes and test again.

Leave to cool and then pot and seal.

Strawberry Cheesecake

Serves 8
Total setting time approx 2 hours

This is a summer favourite with young and old alike, unbeatable when made with in season fruit and served with fresh cream; in comparison, shop-bought versions pale into insignificance.

Ingredients

For the base

- 200g (approx. 7oz) of crushed digestive biscuits
- 3 tbsp melted butter
- 1 tbsp caster sugar
- 1 tbsp of grated lemon rind
- 2 tbsp orange juice

For the strawberry layer

- 1 tbsp lemon juice
- 1 tbsp water
- 2 tsp cornflour with a little orange juice
- 1 kg (approx. 2 lb 3oz) mixed strawberries and raspberries

For the cheesecake layer

- 5 sheets gelatine or 1 ½ sachets
- 450g (approx. 1 lb) cream cheese
- 200g (approx. 7oz) caster sugar
- 200g (approx. 7oz) Greek style yoghurt
- ½ pt cream
- 2 tsp vanilla extract

To serve

- Whipped cream and mint

Method

For the base (biscuit) layer mix all the ingredients together and spread evenly over the base of a 25cm tin that has been greased and lined with clingfilm.

For the fruit layer, place the lemon juice and water in a small saucepan and mix in the cornflour. Bring to the boil, whisking continuously and when the mixture has thickened add the strawberries, raspberries and sugar. Heat the mixture gently to dissolve the sugar, remove from the heat and allow the mixture to cool and thicken.

For the cheesecake mixture soften the gelatine in a little water and lemon juice for 3 to 5 minutes then place over a low heat until the gelatine has completely dissolved.

Meanwhile mix the cream cheese and sugar in a mixer. When the sugar has dissolved add the cream and yoghurt, then add the gelatine and vanilla and mix well.

Pour this mixture over the biscuit base and top with the fruit mix. Place the assembled cheesecake in the fridge and leave to set for approximately 2 hours; it can also be left overnight if desired.

Serve with whipped cream and mint.

Refrigerator Cake

A cake for grown-ups
Serves 8
Total setting time approx 20 minutes

Whenever I make this cake for visitors they only ever ask for a small piece, but being polite only lasts until they reach the last crumbs on their plates, then its back for more.
This is an irresistible treat for the grown-ups!

Ingredients

- 175g (approx. 6oz) of butter, cut into eight pieces, plus extra to grease
- 200g pack of natural glace cherries, halved
- 2 tbsp Kirsch
- 150g (approx. 5.5oz) of dark chocolate (70% cocoa), broken into pieces
- 200g (approx. 7oz) Bourneville chocolate (36% cocoa), broken into pieces
- 100g (approx. 4oz) of golden syrup
- 200g (approx. 7oz) packet of digestive biscuits

Method

Grease a 20cm (approx. 8in) loose bottom round tin and line the base with baking parchment. Put the halved cherries into a bowl, add the Kirsch and then leave to soak.

Put all the chocolate, the butter and the golden syrup into a large microwave-proof bowl and cook for 2 minutes in a 900w microwave oven, adjust the time to suit the power of your microwave. Remove from the microwave and stir, return to the microwave for another 2 minutes, or until the chocolate has melted.

Alternatively, put the chocolate, butter and golden syrup into a bowl and melt over a saucepan of simmering water. It is important to make sure that the bottom of the bowl does not touch the hot water.

Empty the packet of biscuits into a food processor and whiz to crush roughly.

Add half of the Kirsch soaked cherries and all of the crushed biscuits to the melted chocolate and then stir. Pour the mixture into the prepared tin and level the surface.

Arrange the remaining cherries around the edge of the cake and chill for at least 15 minutes before serving.

To serve, remove the cake from the tin and peel off the baking parchment. Cover and store for up to two weeks in the fridge.

Limoncello and Raspberry Semi-freddo

Serves 8

If you do not have any Limoncello you can make a substitute by mixing the juice of half a lemon with a glass of vodka.

Ingredients

For the semi-freddo

- 100g (approx. 4oz) of fresh or frozen (thawed) raspberries
- 85g (approx. 3oz) of golden caster sugar
- 284ml carton of double cream
- 4 tbsp of Limoncello
- 2 x 200ml cartons of crème fraiche

For the coulis

- 225g (approx. 8oz) of fresh or frozen (thawed) raspberries
- 2 tbsp of golden caster sugar
- 2 tbsp of Limoncello
- Extra raspberries, to serve

Method

Line the base of a 1kg loaf tin (19cm x 12cm x 9cm deep) with baking parchment.

For the semi-freddo mash the raspberries and half of the sugar together in a bowl using a fork.

Whisk the cream, the rest of the sugar and the Limoncello together until it forms soft peaks. Beat the crème fraiche briefly until it forms soft peaks like the cream. Gently fold the cream mixture and the crème fraiche together

Pour the mashed raspberries into the cream/crème fraiche mixture and stir just enough to swirl the fruit through the creamy mixture. Pour the contents of the bowl into the prepared loaf tin and smooth the top.

Open freeze the semi-freddo, then cover with clingfilm and tin foil, both the semi-freddo and coulis can be frozen for up to one month.

For the coulis mash the raspberries, sugar and Limoncello together in a bowl with a fork then force the mixture through a sieve.

To serve, thaw the frozen semi-freddo for one hour in the fridge and if the coulis has also been frozen, thaw it out overnight in the fridge. Remove the semi-freddo from the loaf tin and peel off the lining paper. Drizzle the semi-freddo with a little coulis and scatter some raspberries over the top. Serve in slices with the rest of the coulis.

Picnics and Alfresco Dining

For some peculiar reason food eaten alfresco always tastes better than the same food eaten indoors. I love eating outside, especially in the garden on a balmy summer evening when the flowers are in full bloom and the birds are singing their last songs of the day. This can only be improved with a glass of wine and good company.

Picnics and Alfresco Dining

Mushroom Croustades

Serves 6-8
Total cooking time approx 25 minutes

My Wednesday night card-playing friends are always asking me to bring along these little mushroom croustades. The mushroom croustades are always a winner on these occasions, even if I'm not!

Ingredients

- 12 slices of bread

For the filling

- 225g (approx. 8oz) of mushrooms, sliced and diced
- 3 spring onions, sliced
- 50g (approx. 2oz) of butter
- 1 tbsp plain flour
- 237ml (approx. ½ pt) of cream
- 1 tbsp of chopped chives
- Salt and freshly ground black pepper
- Squeeze of lemon juice

For the topping

- 150g (approx. 5oz) white cheddar cheese

Method

Preheat the oven to 220C / 200C fan-oven / Gas mark 7.

Using a 7 ½ cm (approx. 3in) cutter, cut the slices of bread into 24 rounds. Place the bread rounds into 2 x 12 buttered bun trays and toast for about 10 minutes in the hot oven or until slightly brown.

When the bread has toasted, remove trays from the oven and allow them to cool. Reduce the oven temperature to 180C / 160C fan-oven / Gas mark 4.

While the toasted bread rounds are cooling melt the butter in a saucepan and cook the onion and mushrooms until most of the mushroom juice has evaporated.

Add the flour and cook for about 5 minutes then remove from the heat and add the cream, mixing well.

Replace the saucepan on the cooker and stir the contents continuously until it comes to the boil and thickens. Add the lemon juice, chives, salt and pepper mix together and remove from the heat.

Assemble the dish by placing a dessertspoon of the mushroom and onion filling into each of the toasted bread cases. Top each case off with cheese and place in the oven to cook for about 10 minutes at 180C / 160C fan-oven / Gas mark 4. Serve on beds of wild rocket, drizzled with extra virgin olive oil.

Salmon and Smoked Trout Terrine

Serves 8 as a starter

Takes 20 minutes to prepare

I grew up in a fishing village where some of my relatives are fishermen and as a result we always had an abundance of salmon and sea-trout when in season. My mother would make this terrine as a way of using up any left over cooked fish. As well as having access to an abundant supply of fresh fish, our next-door neighbour Danno also smoked fish in his own smoke house. He produced the most wonderful hand crafted smoked salmon and trout that cannot be matched by more commercially made products. He still produces a small amount of smoked fish for family and friends and I always make a point of getting some whenever it's available.

Ingredients

- 800g (approx. 1 ¾ lb) salmon, cooked and flaked
- 100g (approx. 4oz) of smoked trout fillet, flaked
- The juice of 1 ½ lemons
- 2 rounded tsp of powered gelatine
- 237ml (approx. ½ pt) of mayonnaise
- 237ml (approx. ½ pt) of double cream, whipped
- 3 tsp horseradish sauce
- A bunch of fennel or dill, chopped
- 4 – 6 slices of smoked salmon

Method

Line a 2lb loaf tin with clingfilm.

Put the lemon juice into a bowl, sprinkle in the gelatine and leave for about 5 minutes to sponge. Stand the bowl of gelatine mixture in a pot of hot water and gently simmer until the gelatine has melted.

Place the flaked, cooked salmon and flaked smoked trout into a bowl and fold in the mayonnaise, cream and horseradish sauce. Season well and add the chopped fennel or dill.

Add some of the salmon and smoked trout mixture to the pot containing the melted gelatine. Fold the gelatine mixture thoroughly into the rest of the salmon and smoked trout mixture and check the seasoning.

Line the prepared loaf tin with some of the slices of smoked salmon, pour in the salmon and smoked trout mixture and cover with the remaining slices of smoked salmon. Cover loosely with foil and leave to chill overnight in the fridge.

Mozzarella, Mango and Prosciutto Salad

Serves 8 as a starter or 4 as a main course

Ingredients

For the chilli and basil dressing

- 5 tbsp good quality extra virgin olive oil
- 1 tsp sweet chilli sauce
- 3 tbsp chopped, fresh basil leaves
- 2 tbsp of lemon or lime juice

For the salad

- 2 medium sized, ripe mangoes
- 12 slices of Prosciutto
- 3 x 125g mozzarella balls, preferably buffalo
- 100g (approx. 4oz) packet of rocket, wild if possible
- A few small basil leaves to garnish

Method

To make the dressing, whisk the olive oil, chilli sauce, basil and 1 tablespoon of the lemon or lime juice together with a sprinkling of sea salt and freshly ground black pepper. Taste and add more lemon, or limejuice, or seasoning if required.

Prepare the salad by peeling the mangoes and carefully slicing off each fleshy side as close to the stone as possible. Slice the mango flesh lengthways into thin strips. Separate the slices of ham and thinly slice the mozzarella.

Assemble the salad on individual plates or on a single large platter. Pile the rocket in the centre of the plate; arrange a circle of ham and mango around the rocket weaving them in and out of each other. Finish off with a circle of overlapping mozzarella slices then drizzle with the dressing. Before serving, grind over extra black pepper and scatter with basil leaves.

Anne's Tip

If you are not a lover of mozzarella cheese this dish is equally as nice when made with feta cheese instead.

Apple Chutney

Total cooking time approx 30 – 40 minutes

This chutney makes the ideal accompaniment to the Pork and Chicken terrine.

Ingredients

- 910g (approx. 2lb) of cooking apples, peeled and chopped
- 227g (approx. 8oz) of onions, peeled and chopped
- 450g (approx. 1lb) of sultanas
- 680g (approx. 1 ½ lb) of soft brown sugar
- 710ml (approx. 1 ½ pts) of vinegar

Method

Place all the ingredients into a large saucepan and simmer over a moderate heat until the fruit is tender and slightly thickened. This process takes approximately 30 to 40 minutes.

Pot in hot sterilised jars and seal tightly.

Pork and Chicken Terrine

Serves 8

Total cooking time approx 75 minutes

This is a firm family favourite, I often make this dish when all my children are coming home during the summer and we want to eat alfresco.

Ingredients

- 1 onion peeled and finely chopped
- 25g (approx. 1oz) of butter
- 4 cloves of garlic, peeled and chopped
- A handful of mixed, fresh herbs, chopped
- 10 smoked, rind less rashers
- 680g (approx. 1 ½ lb) of pork belly, minced
- 200g (approx. 7oz) of streaky rashers, minced
- 2 eggs
- 100ml (approx. 3 ½ fl oz) of brandy
- 150g (approx. 5oz) of baby spinach leaves and rocket
- 3 tbsp pistachio nuts
- 150g (approx. 5oz) of "no need to soak" apricots
- 2 small, skinless, boneless chicken breast, thinly sliced
- 1 bay leaf

Method

Preheat the oven to 180C / 160C fan-oven / Gas mark 4.

Sweat the onion and butter over a low heat. Add the garlic and chopped herbs, cook for 2 minutes then leave to cool.

Line a 1kg (approx. 2lb) loaf tin with the smoked bacon, leave a few to cover the top.

Put the minced pork belly, the minced bacon, the cooled onion mixture, eggs, brandy, spinach/rocket, nuts and half of the apricots into a bowl and mix thoroughly. Season the mixture well with freshly ground black pepper and a very little sea salt.

Place half of the meat mixture into the prepared loaf tin; then layer the thinly sliced chicken breasts on top; place the remaining apricots on the layer of chicken. Finish assembling the terrine by adding the remainder of the meat mixture and covering it with the last of the rashers and the bay leaf.

Cover the terrine with foil and stand the loaf tin in a tray of hot water, bake in the preheated oven for 1 hour. Uncover and bake for another 15 minutes. Check if the terrine is properly cooked by inserting a clean skewer into the centre of the terrine. If the juices run clear, the dish is cooked.

Leave the terrine overnight to go completely cold, serve sliced with a good plum or apple chutney.

Strawberry and Mascarpone Tart

Serves 6-8

Total cooking time approx 20 minutes

This is one of the most successful, simple tarts that I have baked in Ryelands over the years. It captures all the summer freshness of in-season strawberries and the richness of the mascarpone. The pastry used in this tart has a lemon flavour and the quantity given matches the size of the tart tin used.

Ingredients

For the pastry

- 180g (approx. 6oz) of plain flour
- 110g (approx. 4 ½ oz) of butter
- 25g (approx. 1oz) of icing sugar
- 1 egg white, beaten
- The zest of half a lemon

For the filling

- 30g (approx. 1oz) of caster sugar
- 275g (approx. 10oz) of mascarpone cheese
- 170ml (approx. 6 fl oz) of cream
- Half a vanilla pod, scraped or 1 tsp of vanilla extract
- The zest of half an orange
- 100g (approx. 4oz) of strawberry jam or redcurrant jelly
- 450g (approx. 1 lb) punnet of fresh strawberries, hulled

Method

Preheat the oven to 180C / 160C fan-oven / Gas mark 4.

To make the pastry, rub the flour and butter together, stir in the caster sugar and lemon zest then make a well in the centre.

Mix in the beaten egg yolk and just enough water to form a ball with the flour mixture. Wrap the pastry in clingfilm and leave it to rest in the fridge for 10 or 15 minutes.

Lightly grease a 23cm (approx 9in) round, loose-bottomed tart tin. Roll out the pastry to a size large enough to line the tart tin. Blind bake for 15-20 minutes or until slightly crisp, remove the tart case from the oven and remove the beans.

Brush the tart case with egg white and return to the oven for another 2-3 minutes. Remove the tart case from the oven and allow it to cool.

To make the filling, combine the sugar, mascarpone, cream, vanilla seeds or extract and the orange zest. Whisk the ingredients together until it holds its shape, the consistency will be similar to that of lightly whipped cream.

In a saucepan heat the jam or jelly with a tablespoon of water, force through a sieve to remove any pips. Spread the mascarpone filling in the cooled pastry case and arrange the strawberries on top in a decorative way. Glaze the strawberries with the jam or jelly using a wide pastry brush.

Pavlova

This classic is an all-time favourite, and regardless of changes in taste over the years, it is one recipe that is called on time and time again. The meringue base is very versatile and can be used a base for many other desserts.

Ingredients

For the Pavlova

- 5 egg whites
- 280g (approx. 10oz) of caster sugar
- A pinch of salt

For the filling

- 237ml (approx. ½ pt) of cream, whipped
- Fresh fruit i.e. strawberries, kiwis, etc

Method

Preheat the oven to 160C / 140C fan-oven / Gas mark 3.

Line a swiss-roll tin with parchment and lightly grease with sunflower oil.

Place the egg whites in a clean, dry bowl and whisk until stiff but not dry.

Add the caster sugar to the egg whites one tablespoon at a time and beat for 30 seconds between each application of sugar.

When all the sugar has been added, place the Pavlova mixture onto the prepared swiss-roll tin and spread out to form a 20cm (approx. 8in) circle.

Bake the Pavlova in the preheated oven for 50 minutes then turn off the heat and leave the Pavlova in the oven to cool.

Once the baked Pavlova has cooled, fill the centre with the whipped cream and fresh fruit.

Variations

Peaches and Meringue

Preheat the oven to 160C / 140C fan-oven / Gas mark 3.

Slice up 6 peaches into small pieces and place in an oven-proof dish. Add 50g (approx. 2oz) of light brown sugar and stir together. Top the fruit and sugar with the meringue mix (make to the Pavlova recipe) and bake for about 50 minutes in the preheated oven.

Meringue Roulade

Serves 8
Total cooking time approx 20 minutes

Ingredients

- 4 egg whites
- 210g (approx. 8oz) of caster sugar

Method

Preheat the oven to 160C / 140C fan-oven / Gas mark 3.

Line a swiss-roll tin with greaseproof paper and lightly oil. Make the meringue mixture using the same method and ingredients as for the Pavlova recipe. Tip the meringue mix out onto the swiss-roll tin and spread out in a rectangular shape.

Mix together 1 tbsp of caster sugar and 1 tbsp of ground almonds, sprinkle the mixture over the meringue and bake in the preheated oven for 20 minutes. Take the meringue out of the oven and allow it to cool in the tin.

When the meringue is cold, turn it out onto a clean tea towel and fill it with whipped cream and fresh fruit. Roll the filled meringue up like a swiss-roll, the meringue base remains flexible because it was only baked for 20 minutes. Although this may sound complicated I can assure you that it is easy to do.

Serve the roulade dusted with a mixture of cocoa and icing-sugar.

Anne's Tip

When making meringues of any type, separate the egg whites from the yolks and leave at room temperature for at least 30 minutes before use.

Lemon Butter Sponge

Serves 8
Total cooking time approx 40 minutes

This is one of the true all-time greats that will still be around when my grandchildren have become adults. It continues to be popular with young and old regardless of changes in fashion.

Ingredients

For the sponge

- 175g (approx. 6oz) of margarine
- 175g (approx. 6oz) of self raising flour
- 175g (approx. 6oz) of sugar
- 3 eggs
- ½ tsp of baking powder
- The grated rind of half a lemon

For the filling

- 200g (approx. 8oz) of icing sugar
- 100g (approx. 4oz) of unsalted butter
- The juice and rind of half a lemon
- 2 tbsp of boiling water

Method

Preheat the oven to 180C / 160C fan-oven / Gas mark 4.

Grease a 20cm (approx. 8in) round cake tin.

Place all the sponge ingredients, with the exception of the lemon rind, into a mixing bowl and beat for about two minutes before folding in the grated lemon rind.

Pour the sponge mixture into the greased cake tin and smooth the top. Bake the sponge in the preheated oven for approximately 35-40 minutes or until firm to the touch. When baked, turn the sponge out onto a wire rack and cool.

For the filling, simply place all the ingredients, except for the boiling water, into a bowl and beat until fluffy. Now add the boiling water and beat again until the water has been absorbed.

When the sponge is cold, split it in two and fill with the lemon butter. Dust the top with icing sugar and decorate with lemon and lime rind.

Anne's Tip
You can test whether or not a sponge is fully cooked by inserting a clean metal skewer into the centre of the cake. If the skewer comes out clean, the sponge is cooked.

Cherry and Almond Tart

Serves 8-10
Total cooking time approx 45 minutes

My life long love of cherries comes from visiting my grandmother as a young child and being allowed to eat the ripe, sun warmed cherries straight from her cherry trees. The taste of sun-warmed cherries always brings back memories of my grandmother and what seemed to be endless sunny days.

Ingredients

For the sweet pastry

- 200g (approx. 8oz) of plain flour
- 125g (approx. 4 ½ oz) of butter
- 1 tbsp of icing sugar
- 1 egg
- Cold water

For the almond filling

- 100g (approx. 4oz) of butter, softened
- 100g (approx. 4oz) of caster sugar
- 1 egg and 1 egg yoke, lightly beaten to mix
- 100g (approx. 4oz) of ground almonds
- A pinch of salt
- 375g (approx. 14oz) of cherries, stoned
- Icing sugar, for dusting

Method

Preheat the oven to 190C / 170C fan-oven / Gas mark 5.

Sieve the flour into a bowl and rub in the butter, then add the icing sugar and ground almonds. Mix the egg with 2 tablespoons of cold water and add to the dry mix.

Knead the dough until it is smooth and pulls away from the work-surface easily, this takes about one minute. Shape the dough into a ball, wrap it in clingfilm and chill the dough in the refrigerator for about 30 minutes until firm.

To make the almond filling, cream the butter, add the sugar and beat together vigorously until the mixture is light and soft. Gradually beat in the egg and egg yolk. Finally, stir in the ground almonds and salt, taking care not to over-mix, otherwise the filling will be heavy.

Place a baking sheet low down in the preheated oven. Roll out the pastry dough and use it to line a 25cm (approx. 10in) loose-bottom tart tin. Spread the almond filling evenly in the base of the tart shell. Arrange the cherries, stem side down, in concentric circles on the filling. Chill the filled tart for 10 minutes.

Set the tart in the oven on the heated baking sheet and bake for 40-45 minutes until the pastry has browned and the tart starts to pull away from the sides of the tin. Remove from the oven and leave the tart to cool on a wire rack.

Serve with cream or crème fraiche.

Fruity Cocktails

Pink Grapefruit Ginger and Soda

Serves 2

Ingredients

- 300ml (approx. ½ pt) of ginger ale
- 600ml (approx. 1 pt) of ruby grapefruit or mandarin juice
- 1 litre (approx. 1 ¾ pts) of soda water or 7-Up
- Ice

To serve

Place some ice into a large jug, add the ginger ale and grapefruit juice and pour in the soda water / 7-Up and add some chopped fruit e.g. strawberries, raspberries or apple.

Moscow Mules

Serves 2

Ingredients

- 300ml (approx. ½ pt) of vodka
- 4 limes cut into thin wedges
- 100ml (approx. 3 ½ fl oz) of lime juice
- 750ml (approx. 1 ¼ pts) of ginger ale
- Ice

To serve

Layer a tall jug with ice and lime wedges.

Add the vodka and lime juice and stir, top off with the ginger ale and serve.

Smoothies

Smoothies give great scope for individuality and experimentation; some insist on yoghurt while others are indifferent. For some, breakfast is the time to indulge, for others it makes the perfect late afternoon pick-me-up. Whatever the time of day smoothies are endlessly variable and always rewarding with a great shot of healthy fruit delivered in delicious glassfuls of goodness.

The fruit used varies depending on the season and it is difficult to be precise concerning quantities. A strawberry in July requires little help, in April it is crying out for honey or some other sweetener. Half of the fun of smoothies is playing around with the ingredients and this goes for the sweetness element too. Taste often and adjust accordingly, the one word of caution is restraint – too many ingredients and tastes start to get confused.

The following are a few specific suggestions, but are merely a starting point for experimentation; this is a great opportunity to let your creativity loose. Bananas play a part in most recipes as they help to give the smoothies body. Each of these recipes provides 4 good-sized glasses. Make and serve, smoothies are not known for their keeping qualities.

Passion Fruit and Pineapple

Serves 2

Ingredients

- 1 mango
- 6 passion fruit
- 1 small fresh pineapple
- 1 banana
- 2 cups of chilled orange juice

Method

Place all of the ingredients in a food processor and blend until smooth. The smoothie is best enjoyed immediately after processing. If you would like the smoothie to be cold you can chill or freeze the fruit before use, or simply add ice cubes to the mix. You can also chill your glasses in the freezer before serving; just remember not to leave them there.

This basic method is used for all of our smoothies

Mango Madness

Ingredients

- 4 mangoes
- 2 bananas
- 2 cups of apple or orange juice

Summer Berries

Ingredients

- 2 cups of frozen mixed berries
- 2 bananas
- 2 cups of apple or orange juice or Greek style yoghurt

Strawberry and Orange

Ingredients

- 4 cups of strawberries
- 2 bananas
- 2 cups of orange juice

Grapefruit, Campari and Mint

Ingredients

- The juice of 3 grapefruits
- 1 glass of Campari
- 1 tbsp of finely chopped mint
- 2 bananas

Beaujolais Berries

*Be the host or hostess of the summer with this little number. Be warned,
no matter how much you make it will never be enough!*

Ingredients

- 700g (approx. 1lb 9oz) of strawberries, hulled and halved
- 3 tbsp of golden caster sugar
- A handful of mint leaves plus a few extra
- 1 bottle of Beaujolais

Method

Lay the strawberries in a dish and sprinkle over the caster sugar.

Scatter over a handful of mint leaves and leave to sit for about 30 minutes to allow them to release their juices.

Pour over the Beaujolais and scatter over a few more fresh mint leaves. Leave to rest for another 10 minutes and then serve.

Christmas

Christmas is the time for family and friends to get together to enjoy each others company and relax over a glass of mulled wine. It's also about taking the time together to indulge in long leisurely dinners. However, it also happens to be the busiest time of the year for those responsible for the cooking. This is the one time in a cook's year when they have to be really organised if they wish to have time to enjoy the festivities. If you don't get organised you might find yourself stuck in the kitchen while everyone else is enjoying themselves.

Regardless of changes in fashion, toys or gadgets this is the time when traditional tastes, flavours and smells come to the fore. Here is a selection of recipes that will tide you over the Christmas holidays. They combine the traditional tastes of Christmas with some new ideas that will hopefully make life easier during this busy period.

Christmas

Roasted Vegetable Bread with Garlic

Total cooking time approx 20 - 25 minutes

When your friends and family taste this magnificent bread they will definitely return for more. It is a great addition to any drinks party; cut it into bite-sized pieces and drizzled with olive oil.

Ingredients

- 450g (approx. 1lb) of plain flour
- 1 level tsp of bread soda
- ¼ tsp of salt
- 250g (approx. 9oz) of grated cheese
- About ½ each of a red, green and yellow pepper
- 1 head of garlic, roasted
- 1 fennel bulb, thinly sliced and roasted
- 2-3 tbsp of good quality olive oil
- 250ml (approx. ½ pt) of buttermilk

Method

Preheat the oven to 180C / 160C fan-oven / Gas mark 4.

Sieve the flour, salt and bread soda into a mixing bowl and aerate well.

Add half of the grated cheese and the cloves of garlic and mix well. Make a well in the centre and add the buttermilk to the flour, mix well to make a soft dough.

Turn out the dough onto a floured board and flatten to the size of a normal cake of bread. Place the roasted vegetables on one half of the dough and fold the other half over the roasted vegetables. Flatten the dough again until it is about the size of a normal cake of bread.

Place the flattened bread on an oiled baking sheet, drizzle over with olive oil and sprinkle with the remaining cheese.

Bake in the preheated oven for about 15-20 minutes, or until nice and brown on the bottom. The bread is baked when it sounds hollow when tapped on the base.

Remove from the oven and allow the bread to cool on a wire rack.

Broccoli Soup with Parmesan Toasts

Serves 6
Total cooking time approx 22 minutes

You can make this soup up to two days before you use it, simply store in the fridge and add the cream when reheating.

Ingredients

For the soup

- 25g (approx. 1oz) of butter
- 2 potatoes, peeled and finely chopped
- 1 large onion, peeled and chopped
- 1 head of broccoli, with stalk
- 1 litre (approx. 1 ¾ pt) of hot vegetable or chicken stock
- 170ml (approx. 6 fl oz) of cream
- Sea salt and freshly ground black pepper

For the Parmesan toasts

- 8 slices of good quality white bread
- 75g (approx. 3oz) of parmesan, finely grated

Method

To make the soup, melt the butter in a saucepan and add the potatoes, onion, salt and pepper. Cover the top with greaseproof paper and sweat over a gentle heat for 10 minutes.

While sweating the onion and potato cut the head of broccoli into florets. Using a small knife, remove the skin from the broccoli stalk and then chop the stalk into 1cm pieces. Add the pieces of stalk to the onion and potato and sweat for another 5 minutes.

Add the hot stock to the saucepan and bring to the boil, then throw in the broccoli florets. Boil without a lid for 5 minutes until the florets are soft. Remove from the heat, liquidise, season to taste and add the cream.

For the parmesan toasts toast the bread on both sides. Sprinkle with the grated cheese and pop under a hot grill for 2 minutes or until the cheese melts. Cut the toast into fingers and serve on the side with the soup.

Mixed Melon and Ginger Salad

Serves 6

Okay, it's expensive to pour a bottle of Champagne over melon, but its Christmas after all. For this special occasion consider using your best china cups or crystal glasses.

Ingredients

- 2 ripe Ogen melons, diced or scooped into ball shapes
- 2 ripe Charentais melons, diced or scooped into ball shapes
- 1 or 2 pieces of stem ginger, very finely chopped
- 1 tbsp of syrup from a jar of ginger
- The juice of ½ a lemon
- 2 tbsp of mint leaves, shredded
- A bottle of Champagne, chilled
- Sprigs of mint, to garnish

Method

Place the diced melon into a large bowl, add the remaining ingredients with the exception of the Champagne and stir well.

Cover the bowl with clingfilm and chill in the fridge for at least an hour. Spoon into glass tumblers and top up with the chilled Champagne. Serve immediately garnished with mint leaves.

Anne's Tip
You don't have to use Champagne for this dish; sparkling wine works just as well.

Christmas Salad with Stilton and Pomegranate

Serves 8 as a starter

Pomegranate and stilton is one of those perfect starters for Christmas Day because there is very little effort required in preparing it.

I find that the easiest way to remove the seeds from pomegranates is to cut them in half and lightly beat them with a wooden spoon over a wide bowl.

Ingredients

- 2 oranges
- 2 blood oranges
- 1 pomegranate
- 85g (approx. 3 ½ oz) of wild rocket
- 3 chicory heads (a mixture of red and white), leaves separated
- 2 tbsp of extra virgin olive oil
- 1 tbsp of balsamic vinegar
- 200g (approx. 7oz) of Stilton, sliced
- 75g (approx. 3oz) of walnut halves, toasted
- 50g (approx. 2oz) of pumpkin seeds, toasted

Method

Cut the ends off each orange and blood orange to expose the fruit, then cut all the way around from top to bottom to remove the peel and pith. Slice into rounds and set aside.

Roll the pomegranate on a board or work surface to loosen the seeds, halve and remove the seeds. Layer the rocket, chicory, orange slices and pomegranate seeds on a large platter.

In a small bowl mix together the oil and vinegar, then season and drizzle over the salad. Top with the sliced Stilton and scatter over the walnuts and seeds to serve.

Zesty Cranberry Sauce

Makes 450ml
Total cooking time approx 20 minutes

Cranberry sauce is a vital ingredient of Christmas eating, if any of this sauce is left over after dinner, use it with cold meats.

Ingredients

- 250g (approx. 9oz) of cranberries, fresh or frozen
- 175g (approx. 6oz) of golden granulated sugar
- The finely grated zest and juice of 1 orange
- 3 tbsp of port

Method

Put the cranberries in a saucepan with 5 tbsp of water. Cover the saucepan with a tightly fitting lid and boil for 10 minutes if the berries are fresh, slightly less time for frozen berries or until the skins just start to pop. Add the sugar, grated orange zest, juice and port and stir until the sugar has dissolved.

Bring to the boil, reduce the heat and leave to bubble for 5-8 minutes until the sauce has thickened. Leave to cool and then chill until required. The sauce will keep for 3-4 days in the fridge.

Barbary Duck Breasts in a Plum Sauce with Potato and Leek Cakes

Serves 6
Total cooking time approx 30 minutes

Barbary duck is now available in most supermarkets; if you can't find this type of duck you can use Aylesbury duck instead. This is a great dish for entertaining friends over Christmas; it makes a nice change from turkey and ham. You can make the potato and leek in advance and freeze until needed.

Ingredients

For the duck breast

- 6 Barbary Duck breast fillets marinated in 1 glass of red wine mixed with 2 tbsp of oil and seasoned with salt and pepper.
- 1 glass of red wine
- 2 tbsp of olive oil
- 500g (approx. 1 lb 2 oz) of stoned plums, quartered
- A piece of root ginger, grated
- 2 cinnamon sticks
- 200g (approx. 7oz) of brown sugar
- 200ml (approx. 7 fl oz) of red wine and balsamic vinegar mixed
- 2 tbsp of plum sauce
- Salt and freshly ground black pepper

For the potato and leek cakes

- 1kg (a little over 2 lbs) of peeled potatoes
- 3 finely chopped leeks
- 1 egg

Method

Preheat the oven to 200C / 180C fan-oven / Gas mark 6.

In a large ovenproof dish, mix the red wine with the 2 tablespoons of olive oil, lay the duck breasts in the dish in a single layer to marinate for at least 30 minutes. Turn the duck breasts occasionally.

To make the potato and leek cakes, place the potatoes and leeks in some cold water and season with salt and pepper. Bring to the boil, and when cooked, strain off the water and mash. When the potatoes have cooled enough to handle beat the egg and add to the mix. Correct the seasoning and shape into cakes on a floured board. Leave the potato cakes in the fridge until you are ready to fry them.

Place the ovenproof dish containing the marinade and the duck breasts in a hot oven and cook for about 30 minutes.

While the duck breasts are cooking, make the plum sauce. Place the chopped plums, cinnamon, ginger and sugar in a saucepan over a medium heat and stir until all the sugar is dissolved. Add the vinegar, plum sauce and 500ml (about 1pt) of water. Stir together and cook until the sauce is well thickened, then remove from the heat.

Fry the potato and leek cakes in a mixture of oil and butter, until crisp on both sides. Slice the duck breasts, place a potato cake on a warmed plate and top with sliced duck, pour over some of the plum sauce. Serve with celery and apple that have been cooked together.

Bourbon and Maple Loin of Bacon

Serves 10-12
Total cooking time depends on weight of bacon.

I love a good loin of bacon, especially at Christmas, this sweet glaze perfectly compliments the slightly salty taste of the ham.

Ingredients

- 5.4kg (approx. 12lb) loin of bacon
- 1 head of celery, roughly chopped
- 1 onion, sliced
- A bundle of fresh thyme
- A few peppercorns
- A handful of cloves
- 3 tbsp of ground allspice
- 200ml (approx. 7 fl oz) of maple syrup
- 200ml (approx. 7 fl oz) of bourbon or Irish Whiskey

Method

Weigh the loin of bacon and calculate the simmering time, allow 20 minutes per 450g (approx. 1lb) plus 20 minutes extra. Place the meat in a very large pan, cover with cold water and bring to the boil.

Add the celery, onion, thyme and peppercorns and bring to the boil. Reduce heat and simmer for the calculated amount of time. Drain off the water and leave aside until cool.

Preheat the oven to 180C / 160C fan-oven / Gas mark 4

Once the bacon has cooled enough to handle, remove the outer layer of skin leaving most of the layer of fat intact. Use a sharp knife to score the exposed fat in a diamond pattern but take care not to cut into the meat itself. Retaining the layer of fat has two purposes, it provides an opportunity to decorate the bacon and more importantly it protects the meat from the heat of the oven during glazing. It is very important not to cut into the meat itself as this changes the fibre structure and makes the meat tougher.

In a roasting tin large enough to hold the bacon, pour in enough water to come about 2.5cm (approx. 1in) up the sides. Stud loin of bacon with a clove at the junction of each diamond and then stand it on a wire rack over the water.

Make a paste from the allspice and maple syrup and work in the bourbon. Baste the bacon with some of the paste and bake in the oven for 1 hour, basting at frequent intervals to build up a thick glaze, the water in the roasting tin will evaporate leaving the glaze unscorched. Remove from the oven and allow the bacon to cool before serving.

Buttered Turkey
with Chestnut and Pine Nut Stuffing

Total cooking time depends on weight of bird

From a very young age I was involved with the rearing of the Christmas turkeys and my mother always reared "Bronze" turkeys. The turkey chicks hatched out in June and were ready in December for the turkey market.

As always, it seems to be a case of history repeating itself as I now find myself rearing "Bronze" turkeys for Christmas (family members only!) and my grand daughter helps with the rearing of the turkeys, just as I did at her age. She also knows about the proper care of livestock and very importantly, where her food comes from, a lesson not learned by many today.

If you can get a free-range turkey for Christmas you will be rewarded with good quality meat that has the most wonderful flavour. My method of cooking the Christmas turkey was learned from my grandmother and many of the students at Ryeland House tell me that they have found it to be the easiest way to cook a turkey.

Ingredients

For the stuffing

- 130g (approx. 5oz) of butter
- 1 large onion, chopped
- 1 stick of celery, chopped
- 1 apple, chopped
- 100g (approx. 4oz) of cooked chestnuts, chopped
- 4 tbsp of chopped parsley
- 100g (approx. 4oz) of pine nuts, roasted
- 250g (approx. 9oz) of breadcrumbs
- Salt and freshly ground black pepper

For the flavoured butter

- 250g (approx. 9oz) of butter mixed with parsley, sage, salt and pepper

For the turkey

- A 7kg (approx. 15 lb) fresh "Bronze" or white turkey, free range if possible
- 1 glass of white wine
- 250g (approx. 9oz) of butter, melted
- Salt and freshly ground black pepper
- Some vegetables for the turkey to rest on e.g. carrots or celery

Method

Preheat the oven to 200C / 180C fan-oven / Gas mark 6.

Weigh the turkey to check its weight, calculate the cooking time allowing 20 minutes per 450g (approx. 1lb) and 20 minutes over.

To make the stuffing, melt the butter in a pan, add the onions and celery and cook for about 5 minutes. Add the apple and cook for a further 5 minutes.

Place the breadcrumbs in a large bowl and add the contents of the pan and mix together. Add the remaining ingredients, season well and mix well. Use the stuffing to stuff both the neck-end and cavity of the turkey.

Before roasting the turkey, dry it out with kitchen paper and place a small piece of greaseproof paper in the cavity. Stuff the cavity and neck with the stuffing and push the flavoured butter in between the skin and the breast meat of the turkey.

In a roasting tin large enough to hold the turkey, place two sheets of tin foil, one going north to south and the other going east to west. Place the vegetables in the tray and sit the turkey on top.

Pour over the melted butter and use a pastry brush to make sure that the butter is spread evenly over the bird. Now pour over the white wine and season with salt and pepper. Fold the sheets of tin foil in opposite directions to form a tent-like covering over the turkey.

Place the turkey into the hot, preheated oven for an hour. At the end of the first hour of cooking reduce the oven temperature to 190C / 170C fan-oven / Gas mark 5 and let it remain at that for the remainder of the cooking time. For the final 30 minutes of cooking peel back the tin foil tent to allow the turkey to brown. There is no need to baste the turkey during cooking using this foil method.

Anne's Tip
Make sure that your turkey is out of the oven at least 45 minutes before serving, allowing the turkey to rest for this amount of time makes carving much easier.

Provence Beef Stew

Serves 6
Total cooking time approx 2 ½ hours

This dish can be a real life saver on a busy Christmas Eve, simply make it the day before and reheat to provide a great tasting dish with the minimum of fuss.

Ingredients

For the marinade

- 275ml (approx. ½ pt) of red wine
- 50ml (approx. 2 fl oz) of brandy
- Sprig of thyme and rosemary
- 2 cloves of garlic, chopped
- A few bay leaves
- Black pepper

For the rest

- 1 ½ kg (approx. 3 lb) of sirloin or rib steak cut into chunks
- 4 tbsp of olive oil
- 1 tbsp of flour
- 200g (approx. 7oz) of rashers, chopped
- 2 tbsp of black or green olives, pitted
- 2 carrots, diced
- 2 onions, sliced
- 175g (approx. 6oz) of mushrooms
- 1 tin of chopped tomatoes
- 425ml (approx. ¾ pt) of stock
- Salt and freshly ground black pepper
- Parsley to serve

Method

Place all of the marinade ingredients into a large bowl and mix together. Add the beef pieces and stir, leave to marinate for a couple of hours stirring occasionally.

Preheat the oven to 180C / 160C fan-oven / Gas mark 4.

Lift the meat from the marinade and pat dry using paper kitchen towel. Heat the olive oil in a frying pan and brown the beef in batches. Transfer the browned beef to a casserole dish.

When all the meat has been browned, add the flour to the meat in the casserole dish and toss together.

Brown the onions in the pan then add the mushrooms and garlic, place in the casserole dish. Put the carrots, olives and chopped tomatoes into the casserole and stir.

Lift the herbs from the marinade and add to the meat. Pour the marinade into the pan in which the meat and onion were browned. Bring the liquid to the boil and remove any bits from the pan.

Add the boiled marinade to the casserole dish with enough stock to cover the meat and vegetables. Cover the casserole with greaseproof paper and place the lid on top. Cook the stew in the preheated oven for about 2 hours, or until the meat is tender. Serve topped with chopped parsley.

Roasted Mediterranean Vegetables with Balsamic Dressing

Serves 4
Total cooking time approx 30 minutes

You can cook these vegetables ahead of time, just slightly undercook them and keep them in the roasting tray. Reheat them in the oven for about 20 minutes when required.

Ingredients

- 3 tbsp of olive oil
- 350g (approx. 12oz) of aubergine, trimmed and cut into thin slices
- 350g (approx. 12oz) of courgettes, trimmed and cut into 4cm x 1cm (approx. 1 ½ in x ½ in) batons
- 2 yellow peppers, seeded and cut into large pieces
- 1 large onion, cut into thick wedges
- 2 cloves of garlic, unskinned
- 2 tbsp of balsamic vinegar
- Salt and freshly ground black pepper

Method

Preheat the oven to 220C / 200C fan-oven / Gas mark 7.

Measure the olive oil into a large bowl, add the prepared vegetables and garlic and toss in the oil. Season the vegetables with salt and pepper.

Tip the contents of the bowl into a roasting tin and roast in the preheated oven for about 30 minutes or until golden brown and just tender. Stir once, halfway through cooking.

Peel the roasted garlic, place in a bowl and mash into a paste using the back of a teaspoon. Pour in the 2 tbsp of balsamic vinegar and mix together. Pour over the hot vegetables and serve.

Spiced Red Cabbage

Serves 8
Total cooking time approx 22 - 30 minutes

This is an easy, no-fuss dish and you can still save time by preparing and cooking the cabbage the day before. Simply reheat gently before serving.

Ingredients

- 1kg (approx. 2 lb 4 oz) of red cabbage, cored and finely shredded
- 2 tsp of juniper berries
- 1 tsp of pickling spice
- 1 pear, peeled, cored and chopped
- 300ml (approx. ½ pt) of strong organic cider such as Westons
- 2 tbsp of soft light brown sugar

Method

Put the chopped red cabbage, juniper berries and pickling spice in a saucepan with the chopped pear.

Heat the cabbage gently for 2 minutes before pouring in the cider and adding the sugar. Continue to cook gently for 20 minutes, stirring occasionally.

Season and serve immediately or leave the cabbage to cool before chilling overnight. If you are reheating this dish you may need to add a further 150ml (approx. ¼ pt) of cider to the cabbage.

Baby Brussels Sprouts with Gruyere Sauce

Serves 8
Total cooking time approx 25 minutes

Brussels sprouts get the star treatment with this tasty sauce; they can also be assembled ready to cook the night before use.

Ingredients

- 1kg (approx. 2 lb 4 oz) of baby sprouts, trimmed
- 25g (approx. 1oz) of unsalted butter
- 25g (approx. 1oz) of plain flour
- 600ml (approx. 1 pt) of milk
- 100g (approx. 4oz) of Gruyere cheese, grated

Method

Preheat the oven to 220C / 200C fan-oven / Gas mark 7.

Cook the sprouts in boiling, salted water for 5-7 minutes. Drain and set aside.

Melt the butter in a saucepan; add the flour and cook, stirring, for 1 minute. Gradually add in the milk and stir while bring the mixture to the boil, reduce the heat and simmer for 2 minutes. Stir in about ¾ (75g) of the cheese and season to taste.

Spoon the cooked sprouts into individual ovenproof dishes and pour over the sauce. Sprinkle with the remaining cheese and bake for 15 minutes in the preheated oven until the cheese turns golden and the sprouts are piping hot.

Anne's Tip
Make sure not to over-cook your Brussels sprouts, as this will diminish the flavour.

Baked Walnut Tart

Serves 6
Total cooking time approx 30 minutes

I always love to bake this tart at Christmas. The taste and smell bring back happy memories of my grandmother and me sharing slices of freshly baked walnut tart while we enjoyed the warmth of the range she cooked on.

Ingredients

- A 23cm (approx. 9in) diameter x 4cm (approx. 1 ¾ in) deep, blind-baked pastry case
- 4 tbsp of apricot preserve

For the filling
- 2 eggs, separated
- 2 tbsp of rum
- 125g (approx. 4 ½ oz) of unrefined golden caster sugar
- 2 pinches of cream of tartar
- 125g (approx. 4 ½ oz) of walnut pieces, roughly chopped
- 50g (approx. 2oz) of melted butter

Method

Preheat the oven to 190C / 170C fan-oven / Gas mark 5.

Put the egg yolks, rum and half of the sugar in a mixing bowl and whisk well until the yolks are pale and creamy.

In another mixing bowl whisk the egg whites and cream of tartar (used to prevent the egg white from splitting), add the remaining sugar and continue whisking until firm and glossy.

Spoon the apricot preserve into the base of the cooked flan case and spread evenly using the back of a metal spoon.

Fold the egg whites, chopped walnuts and butter carefully into the whisked egg yolks and then spoon into the prepared flan case. Bake in the preheated oven for about 30 minutes until just set, then remove and cool before cutting. The tart will rise and collapse slightly but this is normal.

Serve with crème fraiche.

Tiramisu Gateau

Serves 10
Takes 20 minutes to prepare

This is a modern take on the traditional Tiramisu and makes a very nice change to traditional cakes over the Christmas period.

Ingredients

- 175g (approx. 6oz) of good quality dark chocolate
- About 300g (approx. 11oz) of Madeira cake
- 150ml (approx. ¼ pt) of strong black coffee
- 5 tbsp of Tia Maria, dark rum or brandy
- 3 x 250g tubs of mascarpone cheese
- 85g (approx. 3 ½ oz) of golden caster sugar
- 425ml (approx. ¾ pt) of double cream
- 85g (approx. 3 ½ oz) of amaretti biscuits

Method

Use a swivel potato peeler to make chocolate curls with about a third of the chocolate. Coarsely grate the rest. Line the base and sides of a 20cm (approx. 8in) round, loose based cake tin with clingfilm.

Cut the Madeira cake into 20 thin slices and use half to line the bottom of the tin, cutting the cake to fit neatly so that there are no gaps. Mix the coffee with the Tia Maria, rum or brandy and sprinkle about a third of the liquid evenly over the cake base.

Beat together two of the tubs of mascarpone with 50g (approx. 2oz) of the sugar. Whip 300ml (approx. ½ pt) of the cream and then fold it into the cheese. Spoon half of this mixture over the cake base spreading it evenly using the back of a metal spoon. Sprinkle with half of the grated chocolate.

Crumble the amaretti biscuits into small pieces and scatter evenly over the chocolate. Sprinkle over another third of the coffee liqueur, then add the remaining mascarpone mixture, smooth and top off with the rest of the grated chocolate.

Cover the top with clingfilm and chill overnight. Chill the chocolate curls on a separate plate covered loosely with clingfilm.

Up to 2 hours before serving, uncover the cake and invert it onto a flat serving plate, carefully remove the cake tin and peel off the clingfilm. Soften the remaining mascarpone with the remaining sugar, whip the rest of the cream and fold into the cheese. Spread this mixture over the top and sides of the cake, and then scatter the chilled chocolate curls over the top. Cut into slices to serve.

The Best Mango and Raspberry Trifle Ever

Serves 8

*Christmas is just not Christmas without a good trifle; for this version use
frozen raspberries and your own homemade custard.*

Ingredients

For the trifle

- 2 mangoes
- The finely grated zest and juice of 1 lime
- 150g (approx. 5oz) punnet of raspberries
- 1 whole swiss roll (vanilla and jam), sliced
- 450ml (approx. 1pt) of fresh custard
- 5 tbsp of crème de cassis
- 400ml (approx. 14 fl oz) of softly whipped fresh cream
- To decorate – some pomegranate seeds or cherries, chocolate curls and icing sugar

For the custard

- 6 egg yolks
- 1 tsp of cornflour
- ½ tsp of vanilla extracts
- 1 tbsp sugar
- 450ml (approx. 1pt) of cream/milk or mixture of both

Method

For the custard, pour the cream or milk into a saucepan and bring to the boil. While the cream is heating whisk the egg yolks, sugar, vanilla extracts and cornflour together in a large bowl.

When the cream has reached boiling point remove from the stove and add to the egg mixture whisking all the time. Return the mixture to the saucepan and whisk over a low heat until thickened.

To make the trifle, peel the mangoes, slice one of them into thin strips and combine with the lime zest. Cut away the flesh from the remaining mango and puree in a food processor with the lime juice until smooth. Gently stir the mixture into the mango strips with the raspberries.

Arrange the slices of swiss roll around the base and sides of a bowl. Drizzle over the crème de cassis and top with the mango and raspberry mixture. Finish with any remaining pieces of swiss roll.

Pour over the custard and leave in the fridge to set, preferably overnight.

Place the whipped cream on top and decorate with the pomegranate seeds or cherries, chocolate curls and lemon balm if available. Dust with icing sugar.

Mum's Mince Pies

Makes 12-14 large or 20-22 small
Total cooking times approx 20 minutes for large pies and 14 minutes for small pies

My mother always made her own mincemeat in September; she said that it needed at least a couple of months to mature before use at Christmas. Her mincemeat was always perfect so if you can make your own, go ahead or buy some homemade mincemeat from your local farmers' market.
If you like large mince pies, use ordinary muffin tins for baking or for a smaller size use mini-muffin tins.

Ingredients

For the pastry
- 300g (approx. 11oz) of plain flour
- 75g (approx. 3oz) of caster sugar
- 175g (approx. 6oz) of unsalted butter
- 1 medium egg yolk
- Mincemeat for filling

For the topping
- 150g (approx. 5oz) of white marzipan
- 1 medium egg white, lightly beaten
- Caster sugar for sprinkling

Method

Preheat the oven to 210C / 190C fan-oven / Gas mark 6.

Sift the flour and sugar into a mixing bowl then rub in the butter until the mixture has the appearance of fine breadcrumbs. Work in the egg yolk to form a smooth dough. Wrap the dough in clingfilm and chill for about 15 minutes.

Divide the pastry in half and roll out thinly, cut out circles big enough to suit the size of the muffin tins you are using. Use the pastry rounds to line the muffin tins, repeat the process with the second half of the pastry.

Divide the mincemeat evenly between the pastry cases. Roll out the marzipan and cut out star or circular shapes and place on top of the pies. Brush the marzipan with the egg white and sprinkle with caster sugar.

Bake the pies in the preheated oven for 18-20 minutes or until crisp and golden. Allow the pies to cool for about 5 minutes before tipping them out onto a wire rack and quickly turning them the right way up. This is much easier and does less damage than trying to prise them out of the tins with a knife.

Anne's Tip
The pies can be made at least a month in advance and frozen raw.
Thaw completely before baking.

Mulled Wine

I love the smell of mulled wine because I think it is one of the defining smells of Christmas and I always try to make some when friends or family visit us during Christmas.

Ingredients

- 1 bottle of red wine
- ½ a carton of orange juice
- 148ml (approx. 5 fl oz) of water
- 90ml (approx. 3 fl oz) of brandy
- 50g (approx. 2oz) of brown sugar
- 1 orange and 1 lemon, sliced
- 2 cinnamon sticks
- 4 or 5 cloves

Method

Place the sugar, cloves, water and cinnamon sticks in a saucepan and bring to the boil.

Simmer for 10 minutes and then add the wine, brandy and orange juice. Keep warm and serve with orange slices and cinnamon sticks.